SAP SRM Extended Classic Cookbook

By Shaz Khan

Including SAP SRM-EBP Extended Classic Configuration Guide

For SRM 4.0/EBP 5.0

Please visit our website at www.sapcookbook.com

ISBN 9753052-7-1

TABLE OF CONTENTS

EBP Extended Classic Configuration Guide

This document covers the necessary steps to configure the SRM 4.0 /EBP 5.0 and R/3 4.6c (or greater) system in an Extended Classic scenario. Some of the customizing settings presented in this document are meant to serve as examples only and might not reflect how your organization's specific values. The configuration steps should be completed according to the sequence of the chapters (unless otherwise specified). This configuration guide is by no means exhaustive and does not cover the integration of other SRM components that complement the SRM system such as Sourcing Cockpit, Contract Management, and Supplier Self Services (SUS).

1.) Post-Processing Basis

Team Responsible:	**Basis**
Transportable:	**N/A**

- Internet Transaction Server (ITS) settings are made via SICF
- The start URL (Uniform Resource Locator) for the *SAP Enterprise Buyer* system is: **http://<host_name>.<domain_name>:<port>/scripts/wgate/bbpstart/!?~language=<language>** whereby **<language>** = en
- Define logical systems and RFC connections via SM59
- Create RFC user to pass data from EBP to R/3
- Make entries needed for generating application URLs in table TWPURLSVR
- Execute Workflow Customizing via transaction code SWU3
- Set control parameters
- Start the Internet Pricing Configurator (IPC).

- Configure CCM 1.0
- Create RFC connection to TREX6.1 Server.

2.) General Settings

2.1) Scheduling Reports

Team Responsible:	**Basis**
Transportable:	**Yes**

Use
In order for EBP to run successfully, certain reports need to be scheduled and executed in order for the EBP system to determine if follow-on documents have been generated for a shopping cart request. The reports such as BBP_GET_STATUS_2 provide status of the shopping cart requests and purchase orders to determine if any follow-on documents such as goods receipts and invoices have been posted in the backend system.

Procedure
Schedule the following reports via transaction code SM37:

Function	**Report Name**	**Frequency**	**Description**
Update requirement coverage requests	BBP_GET_STATUS_2	Schedule this report to run every 2 – 5 minutes.	Schedule this report to run daily in the *Enterprise Buyer* system, so that information on the status of purchase requisitions, purchase

Function	Report Name	Frequency	Description
			orders, and reservations is up-to-date.
Interval for update check	CLEAN_REQREQ_UP	Schedule this report to run every 2 – 5 minutes.	Updating of documents (purchase requisitions, purchase orders, reservations) is executed asynchronously in the backend system. You can only process the requirement coverage request in the *Enterprise Buyer* system further after the update has been carried out. At the interval defined by you in Customizing, the system checks whether the

Function	Report Name	Frequency	Description
			documents have been updated and thus if you can further process the requirement coverage request.
Currencies and exchange rates	BBP_GET_CURRENCY, BBP_GET_EXRATE	*Schedule this report to run weekly*	To ensure that the currencies and exchange rates in the *Enterprise Buyer* system match those in the backend system, you must schedule **both** reports. Make sure that the reports are run each time that the currencies and exchange rates are changed in the backend system.

Function	Report Name	Frequency	Description
Send Workflow Email Notifications	RSWUWFMLEC	*Schedule this report to run every 1-3 minutes*	The report sends notifications for work items via email to e-mail recipients. E-mails are only sent to those users for which the user attributes (FORWARD_WI) '*Flag: Forward work item"* are maintained via tcode PPOMA_BBP.
Selection and processing of Purchase Order Output	RSPPFPROCESS	If the purchase orders shall be transferred to the vendors such as email, auto-fax, or XML, *schedule this*	This report will submit purchase orders to a vendor via email or any other communication method.

Function	Report Name	Frequency	Description
		report to run every 2-5 minutes.	
Selection of Purchase Orders	RSBBPPPFSEL	Manual	Selected individuals can run this report to manually output purchase orders
Improve performance in the organizational plan	RHBAUPAT	*Schedule the report to run once daily every night.*	The report carries out inheritance of attributes and saves the attributes so that they can be accessed directly.

2.2) Set/Verify Control Parameters

Team Responsible:	**Basis – Setup** **Functional Configuration - Validation**
Transportable:	**Yes**

Use

The Spooler is used to communicate EBP data to the R/3 system. The spooler must be active and running in order for EBP Purchase Orders to be replicated to the backend system.

Procedure

SAP SRM Menu	*IMG ? Supplier Relationship Management ? SRM Server ? Technical Basic Settings ? Set Control Parameters*
Transaction code	SPRO

Verify the following settings in the 'Entry' column for each row. If the values do not exist under the 'Entry' column, please notify Basis to add the appropriate values.

Key Control Description	Description	Entry
SPOOL_JOB_USER	User that executes spool job	SRMRFCUSR
SPOOL_LEAD_INTERVAL	Interval by which the retry time increments	60
SPOOL_MAX_RETRY	Max. number of retries for writing BAPIS	5

2.3) Start Application Monitors

Team Responsible:	**Basis**
Transportable:	**No**

Use

Application monitors are started during the installation of your *SAP Enterprise Buyer* system. This will display any system error that may occur when running an *SAP Enterprise Buyer* application.

Procedure

Perform this step once after the installation of *SAP Enterprise Buyer*.

SAP SRM Menu	*Supplier Relationship Management ? SRM Server ? Cross-Application Basic Settings ? Start Application Monitors*
Transaction code	SPRO

2.4) Validate Internet Pricing and Configurator (IPC) is Active

Team Responsible:	**Basis – Setup** **Functional Configuration - Validation**
Transportable:	**No**

Use

The Internet Pricing and Configurator (IPC) is an SAP Java add-on component for Enterprise Buyer and is requirement for the SRM/EBP Extended Classic Scenario. Since purchase orders are generated locally in the EBP system in Extended Classic, the IPC engine facilitates adding pricing condition records such as discount (absolute, quantity, percentage) to any line item in an EBP purchase order, which mimics the functionality that would be available if purchase orders were created directly in the SAP R/3 backend system.

Procedure

SAP SRM Menu	*Supplier Relationship Management ? SRM Server ? Cross-Application Basic Settings ? Pricing ? Check Technical and Customizing Settings for Conditions*
Transaction code	SPRO

Validate: Click Execute. Verify that the IPC Pricing is active as in the report results screenshot below.

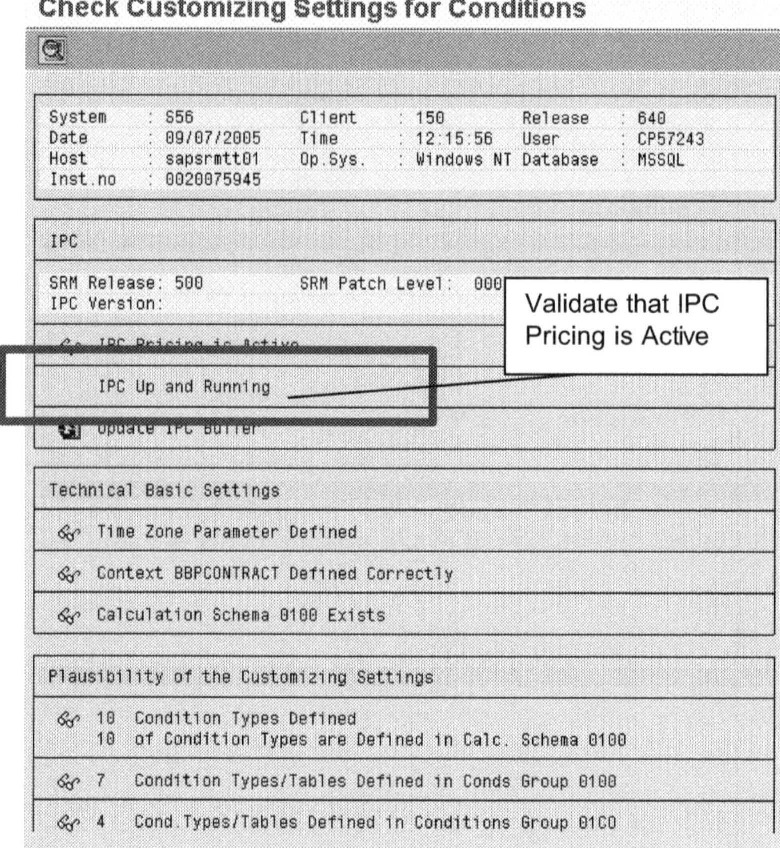

2.5) Validate SAPConnect for Sending Internet Mails is Active

Team Responsible:	**Basis – Setup** **Functional Configuration - Validation**
Transportable:	**No**

Execute a shopping cart approval workflow to validate that email are sent for workflow work items.

2.6) Extended Classic Scenario – Specific Settings

Team Responsible:	**Functional Configuration**
Transportable:	**Yes**

Use
The default implementation mode for EBP after installation is Classic. In order to activate the 'Extended Classic Scenario' and generate local purchase orders in EBP, you must activate the extended classic scenario in EBP.

Procedure

SAP SRM Menu	*Supplier Relationship Management ? SRM Server ? Cross-Application Basic Settings ? Activate Extended Classic Scenario*
Transaction code	SPRO

Setting: Set the 'Extended Classic Scenario Active' checkbox and click 'Save'.

2.7) Tax Calculation Settings

Team Responsible:	**Functional Configuration**
Transportable:	**Yes**

Use

Sales tax will be automatically calculated in *SAP Enterprise Buyer* based on the R/3 tax settings. The system calculates tax when a shopping cart or purchase order is created.

You can use the tax calculation functions in the following applications:

• Shop
The system determines a tax indicator. You can change the default tax indicator. You can display the tax amounts for each item individually and as total amount. You can define whether the system takes tax amount into account in the approval process.

• Create Purchase Order
You can change the default tax indicator. The system calculates the tax on the basis of the current data. You can display the tax amounts for each item individually and as total amount.

Procedure

SAP SRM Menu	*Supplier Relationship Management SRM Server ? Cross-Application Basic Settings ? Tax Calculation ? Determine System for Tax Calculation*
Transaction code	SPRO

Settings:

1.) Determine System for Tax Calculation

SAP R/3 system - (Tax calculation takes place in the financial accounting system)
Since you are currently using a *SAP R/3* financial accounting system, EBP will utilize the existing tax calculation provided by the *R/3* system. If your

R/3 system is integrated with a third party tax calculation package such as Vertex or Taxware, the tax rate and subsequent value is derived from the ship-to address for the line item. If the ship-to address is changed, the tax rate will dynamically update based on street code, zip code, and state.

Select 'Tax Calculation Occurs in R/3' radio button. Click Save.

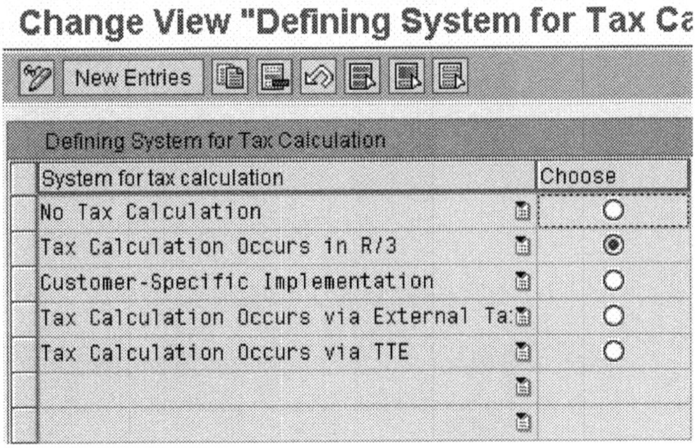

Change View "Defining System for Tax Ca

New Entries

Defining System for Tax Calculation

System for tax calculation	Choose
No Tax Calculation	○
Tax Calculation Occurs in R/3	◉
Customer-Specific Implementation	○
Tax Calculation Occurs via External Ta:	○
Tax Calculation Occurs via TTE	○

2.) Define Tax Codes

SAP SRM Menu	*Supplier Relationship Management ? SRM Server ? Cross-Application Basic Settings ? Tax Calculation ? Enter Tax Code*
Transaction code	SPRO

Setting: Enter two tax codes. In this example, we will enter tax codes I0 and I1. Make the following entries according to the screenshot below. Note: The 'Tax Description' field is displayed on the

shopping cart or purchase order, so please make the field descriptive.
Select the 'Sales Tax' option under Tax Category.
In this sample configuration, we will make all items in a shopping cart default as Taxable (I1 – Regular Tax).

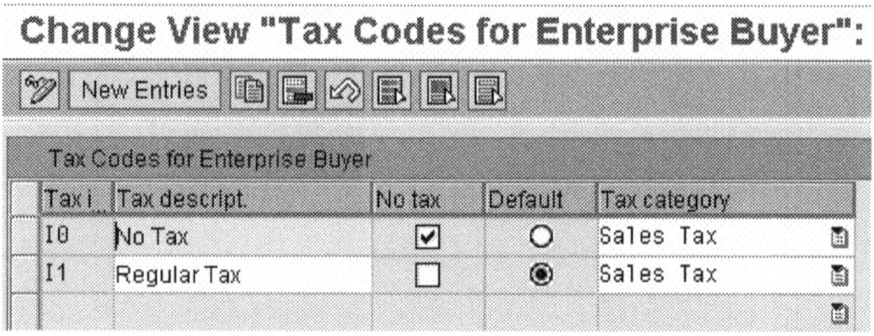

Change View "Tax Codes for Enterprise Buyer":

New Entries

Tax Codes for Enterprise Buyer

Tax i...	Tax descript.	No tax	Default	Tax category
I0	No Tax	☑	○	Sales Tax
I1	Regular Tax	☐	◉	Sales Tax

2.8) Message Configuration

Team Responsible:	**Functional Configuration**
Transportable:	**Yes**

Use
Certain messages will be configured to be switched off or displayed as warning or error messages. Currently, there has only been one message identified to be switched off during the EBP shopping cart creation process AM-228

Procedure

SAP SRM Menu	*N/A*
Transaction code	OBA5

Settings:

1.) Select 'AM' as the application area and click 'Enter'
2.) Select 'New Entries' and enter message number 228. Select 'Switch Off' for both the Online and Batch columns.
3.) Click Save.

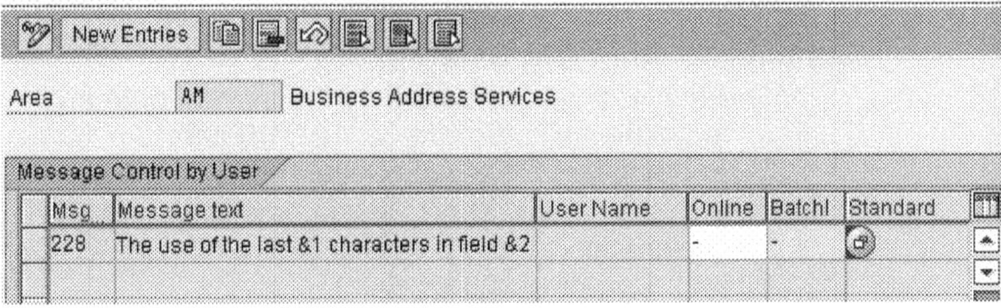

2.9) Create Root Org. Unit

Team Responsible:	**Functional Configuration**
Transportable:	**No, however EBP Org. Structure can be ALE'd over via standard IDoc to different clients**

Use
In order for the EBP system to function, you must create an org. structure with organizational units and persons. This step will cover creating the top-level org. unit node for the org structure, as well as the vendor root node and the purchasing organization root node.

Procedure

SAP SRM IMG Menu	*Supplier Relationship Management ? SRM Server ? Cross-Application Basic Settings ? Organizational Management ? Create Organizational Plan*
Transaction code	PPOCA_BBP

Settings for Root Org Unit:

1.) Enter the validity period as the current date and leave the valid to date as '12/31/9999'.
2.) In the 'Basic Data' tab for the new org unit enter the appropriate Short Description and Long Description for the Org Unit (For example: ROOT and 'Corporate Enterprise')
3.) Click the 'Address' tab and enter a valid address for the root org. unit (for example, the global headquarters address for your company)
4.) Click Save.

Settings for Vendor Root Org. Unit:

SAP SRM IMG Menu	*Supplier Relationship Management ? SRM Server ? Cross-Application Basic Settings ? Organizational Management ? Maintain Organizational Plan*
Transaction code	PPOMA_BBP

1.) Highlight the root org unit and click the 'Create' icon
2.) Enter the validity period as the current date and leave the valid to date as '12/31/9999'.
3.) In the 'Basic Data' tab for the new org unit enter the appropriate Short Description and Long Description for the Org Unit (For example: VEND and Vendor Root)

4.) Click the 'Address' tab and enter a valid address for the root org. unit (for example, the global headquarters address for your company)
5.) Click Save.

Settings for Purchasing Organization Org. Unit:

SAP SRM IMG Menu	*Supplier Relationship Management ? SRM Server ? Cross-Application Basic Settings ? Organizational Management ? Maintain Organizational Plan*
Transaction code	PPOMA_BBP

1.) Highlight the root org unit and click the 'Create' icon
2.) Enter the validity period as the current date and leave the valid to date as '12/31/9999'.
3.) In the 'Basic Data' tab for the new org unit enter the appropriate Short Description and Long Description for the Org Unit (For example: CENTPURORG and Central Purchasing Organization)
4.) Click the 'Address' tab and enter a valid address for the root org. unit (for example, the global headquarters address for your company)
5.) In the 'Function' tab, and click the 'Purchasing Organization' checkbox. Enter the name of the purchasing organization in the field next to the 'Corresponding' label. (Example: POG1)
6.) Click Save

In Step 5 above, when selecting the 'Purchasing Organization' checkbox, you must also select the 'Company' checkbox and leave the other values blank. This step is required in order for you to be able to output the EBP Purchase Order Smart Form.

3.) System Connections

3.1) Define backend systems

Team Responsible:	**Functional Configuration**
Transportable:	**No**

Use
This section describes the settings that must be made to connect one or more backend systems to *SAP Enterprise Buyer.*

Prerequisites

1) Backend systems have been defined as unique logical systems.
2) For each backend system:
   a) You have specified the logical system.
   b) You have specified the RFC destination.
   c) You have created a second RFC connection for the same backend system (for account assignment search help in the backend system, for example).
3) You have defined how FI data is to be validated.
4) You have replicated/created the product categories.

Procedure

SAP SRM Menu	*Supplier Relationship Management ? SRM Server ? Technical Basic Settings ? Define Backend Systems*
Transaction code	SPRO

Setting:

a.) Enter the logical system, destination and system type of the SRM system. The system type of the SRM system should be 'Local B2B System' and the 'Local' checkbox should be checked.

b.) Enter the logical system, destination and system type of the backend system. The system type of the backend system should be 'R/3 system – Version 4.70' and select the RFC indicator in the 'RFC' checkbox. Enter the logical system ID in the 'RFC Destination' field.

Note: If you are using the Catalog Content Management system (CCM) and the CCM Catalog Authoring Tool is installed on a separate server than the EBP 5.0 Application (SRM Server 5.0), you will also need to define a RFC destination for the CCM connection.

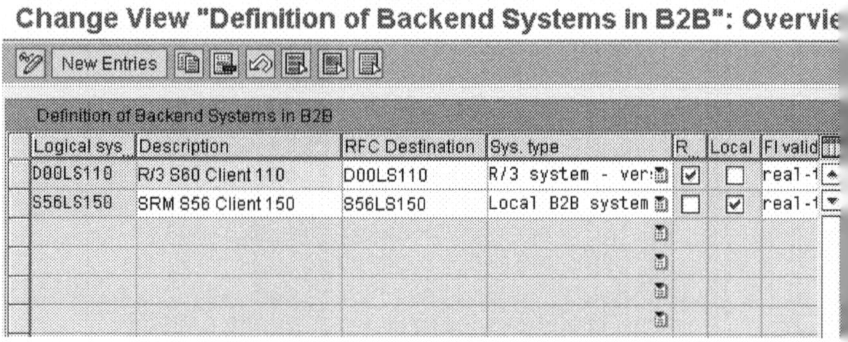

Change View "Definition of Backend Systems in B2B": Overvie

New Entries

Definition of Backend Systems in B2B

Logical sys.	Description	RFC Destination	Sys. type	R...	Local	FI valid
D00LS110	R/3 S60 Client 110	D00LS110	R/3 system - ver:	☑	☐	real-t
S56LS150	SRM S56 Client 150	S56LS150	Local B2B system	☐	☑	real-t

3.2) Define backend systems for product category

Team Responsible:	**Functional Configuration**
Transportable:	**Yes, however system names must be changed in each EBP client build**

Use

In order for the extended classic scenario to function correctly, a backend system needs to be defined for all product categories.

Procedure

SAP SRM Menu	*Supplier Relationship Management ? SRM Server ? Technical Basic Settings ? Define Backend System for Product Category*
Transaction code	SPRO

Setting

- Enter a wildcard (*) in the 'Category ID' field.
- In the 'Target System' field, enter the R/3 backend system (validate that the source system is also populated automatically from the Target System entry.

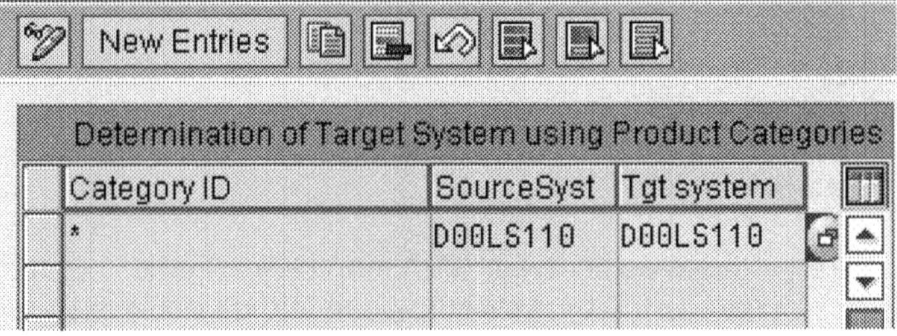

4.) Define Middleware Parameters

Team Responsible:	**Basis**
Transportable:	**No**

Use

In order to replicate data from the backend R/3 system (or any other system), the middleware parameters in EBP must be defined and the data filters must be entered as to which data will be imported.

Procedure

SAP SRM Menu	*Supplier Relationship Management ? SRM Server ? PUT IN REST OF PATH*
Transaction code	SMOEAC

Step 1: Specify the R/3 backend system for middleware download in EBP

Setting:

a.) Chose object type “Site” then click “Create”. Enter name of SAP system to point to then enter the description and choose R/3 for “type”. Then click on “Site Attributes button.

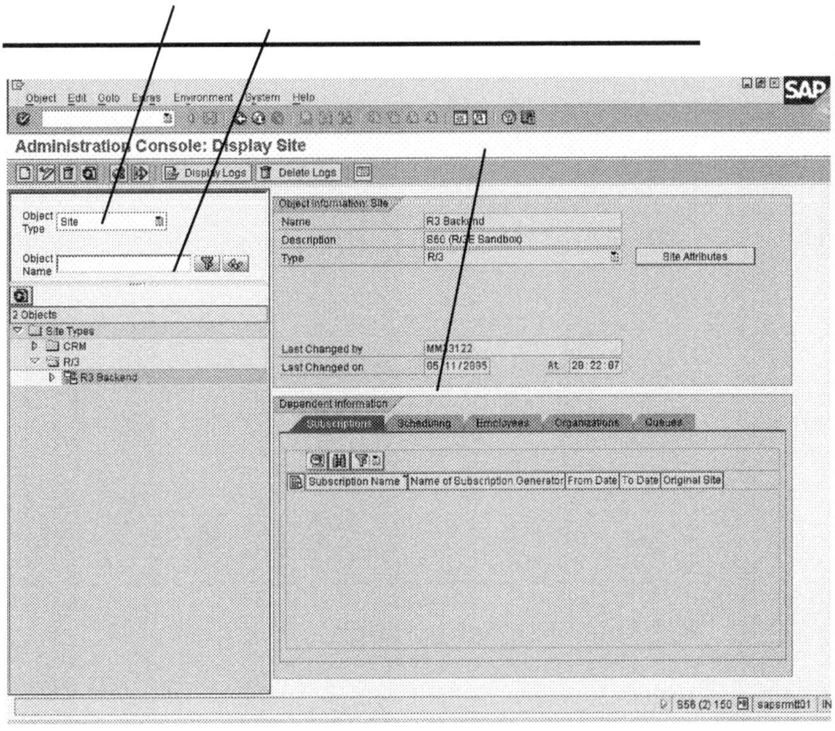

b.) Then, choose the R/3 backend system name from dropdown and click the 'Green' checkmark.

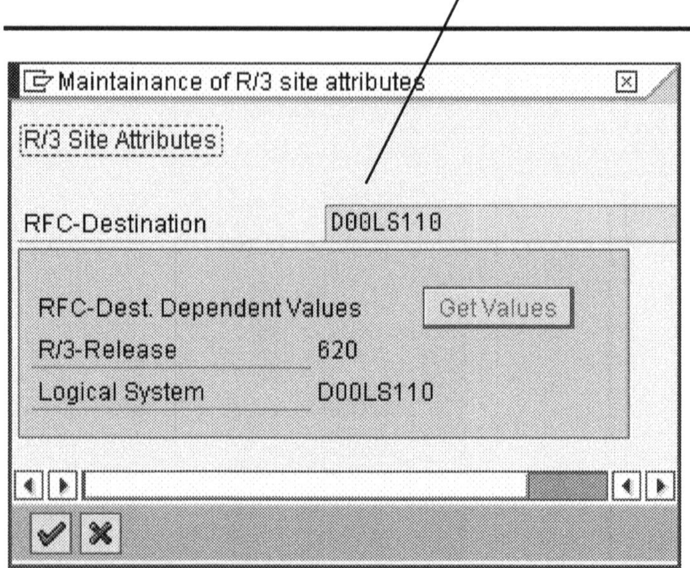

R/3 Specific Configuration

Use
Per OSS Notes **430980 and 720819,** special settings will need to be made in the R/3 system for the following tables CRMCONSUM, CRMSUBTAB, CRMRFCPAR, CRMPAROLTP.

Procedure

a.) **Transaction Code:** SM30 (in the R/3 system) – Enter table CRMCONSUM

Verify the 'SRM' entry has been configured by the Basis team:

Display View "Possible Users of R/3 Adapter Functionality": Overview

Possible Users of R/3 Adapter Functionality

User	Ac	Description	Q_Prefix
CRM	✓	CRM	R3A
MDM	✓	MASTER DATA MANAGEMENT	MDM
SRM	✓	S56 SRM CONSUMER	SRM

b.) Transaction Code: SM30 (in the R/3 system) – Enter table CRMSUBTAB

Verify the following 'SRM' entries are made in the table.

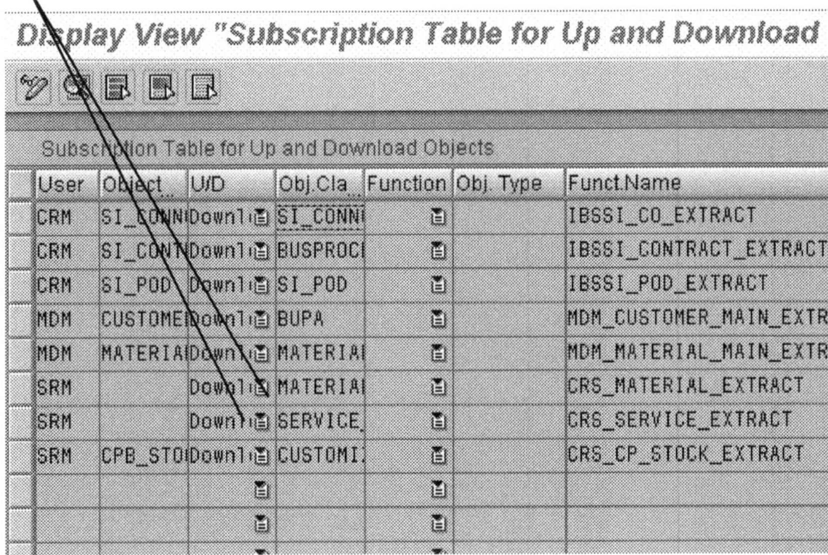

Display View "Subscription Table for Up and Download

Subscription Table for Up and Download Objects

User	Object	U/D	Obj.Cla	Function	Obj. Type	Funct.Name
CRM	SI_CONN	Downl	SI_CONN			IBSSI_CO_EXTRACT
CRM	SI_CONT	Downl	BUSPROC			IBSSI_CONTRACT_EXTRACT
CRM	SI_POD	Downl	SI_POD			IBSSI_POD_EXTRACT
MDM	CUSTOME	Downl	BUPA			MDM_CUSTOMER_MAIN_EXTR
MDM	MATERIA	Downl	MATERIA			MDM_MATERIAL_MAIN_EXTR
SRM		Downl	MATERIA			CRS_MATERIAL_EXTRACT
SRM		Downl	SERVICE_			CRS_SERVICE_EXTRACT
SRM	CPB_STO	Downl	CUSTOMI			CRS_CP_STOCK_EXTRACT

c.) Transaction Code: SM30 (in the R/3 system) – Enter table CRMRFCPAR

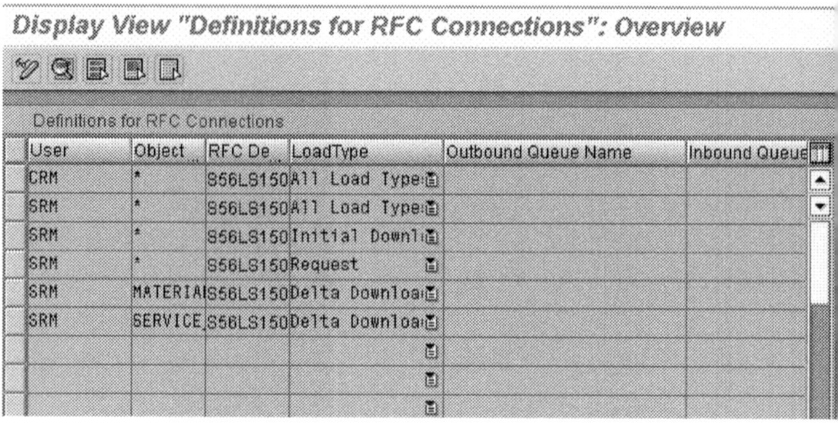

Display View "Definitions for RFC Connections": Overview

Definitions for RFC Connections

User	Object	RFC De..	LoadType	Outbound Queue Name	Inbound Queue
CRM	*	S56LS150	All Load Type		
SRM	*	S56LS150	All Load Type		
SRM	*	S56LS150	Initial Downl		
SRM	*	S56LS150	Request		
SRM	MATERIAL	S56LS150	Delta Downloa		
SRM	SERVICE	S56LS150	Delta Downloa		

d.) **Transaction Code:** SM30 (in the R/3 system) – Enter table CRMPAROLTP

NOTE: BASIS added the line for **CRM_FILTERING_ACTIVE** for the parameter "MATERIAL" for the "SRM" user.

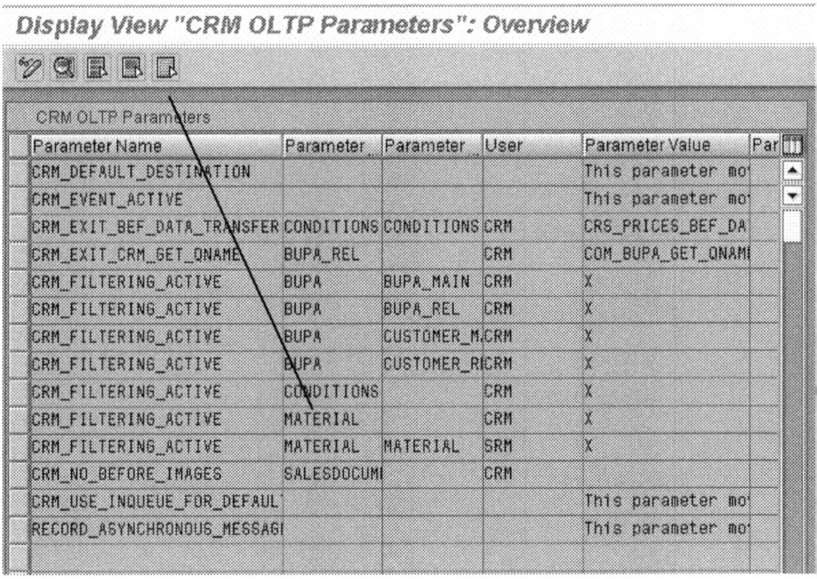

Display View "CRM OLTP Parameters": Overview

CRM OLTP Parameters

Parameter Name	Parameter	Parameter	User	Parameter Value	Par
CRM_DEFAULT_DESTINATION				This parameter mo	
CRM_EVENT_ACTIVE				This parameter mo	
CRM_EXIT_BEF_DATA_TRANSFER	CONDITIONS	CONDITIONS	CRM	CRS_PRICES_BEF_DA	
CRM_EXIT_CRM_GET_ONAME	BUPA_REL		CRM	COM_BUPA_GET_ONAM	
CRM_FILTERING_ACTIVE	BUPA	BUPA_MAIN	CRM	X	
CRM_FILTERING_ACTIVE	BUPA	BUPA_REL	CRM	X	
CRM_FILTERING_ACTIVE	BUPA	CUSTOMER_M	CRM	X	
CRM_FILTERING_ACTIVE	BUPA	CUSTOMER_R	CRM	X	
CRM_FILTERING_ACTIVE	CONDITIONS		CRM	X	
CRM_FILTERING_ACTIVE	MATERIAL		CRM	X	
CRM_FILTERING_ACTIVE	MATERIAL	MATERIAL	SRM	X	
CRM_NO_BEFORE_IMAGES	SALESDOCUM		CRM		
CRM_USE_INQUEUE_FOR_DEFAUL				This parameter mo	
RECORD_ASYNCHRONOUS_MESSAG				This parameter mo	

EBP Specific Middleware Configuration

Use

Per OSS Notes **632223 and 720819,** special settings will need to be made in the R/3 system for the following table SMOFPARSFA.

Procedure

Transaction Code: SM30 (in the R/3 system) – Enter table SMOFPARSFA

Make the following settings in the table. Make sure the user ‘SRM’ is entered in the ‘Param. Value’ field.

Display View "Middleware Parameter": Detail

Key	MCRM
Parameter Name	MCRM_CONSUMER
Param. Name 2	
Param. Name 3	

Middleware Parameter

User	<USERNAME>
Param. Value	SRM
Param. Value 2	
Comment	
Created by	
Modification Date	
Changed by	
Date of Creation	

IMPORTANT √

Before any data is replicated from R/3 to EBP, please execute the following steps:

a.) Run transaction SE38 and execute report **BBP_PRODUCT_SETTINGS_MW**

b.) Enter the value 'SRM' in the User field. Select 'Service Product Active', and check the 'Test Mode' checkbox. Click 'Execute'.
c.) A report should be generated similar to the one below.
d.) Click the 'Back' icon and deselect the 'Test Mode' checkbox. Click 'Execute' to generate the report and activate the middleware settings.
e.) Report will be generated as in Step C.

```
Middleware Settings for Product for SRM Systems

Settings Log:                        EBP Without CRM
               ***** Test Mode *****

Set Middleware Objects to Active/Inactive
All Business Objects Except MATERIAL and DNL_PLANT Will Be Set to Inactive
All Customizing Objects Except DNL_CUST_PROD0/_PROD1 Will Be Set to Inactive
All Condition Objects Will Be Set to Inactive
Objects SERVICE_MASTER and DNL_CUST_SRVMAS Will Also Be Activated

User of Download Objects Will Be Adjusted (Table SMOFINICON)

Object:      MATERIAL
Following Tables Will Be Deactivated:
  MLAN
  MVKE
  STXH
  STXL

Object:      DNL_CUST_PROD1
Following Tables Will Be Deactivated:
  T179
  T179T

Middleware Objects Will Be Regenerated


EBP Will Be Flagged As Active Application (Table SMOFAPPL)
CRM Will Be Flagged As Inactive Application (Table SMOFAPPL)


Customizing Indicator 'Multiple-Backends' Set (Table COMC_HIERARCHY)
```

5.) Configure Number Ranges and Document Types

5.1) Define Number Ranges in EBP

Team Responsible:	**Functional Configuration**
Transportable:	**Yes*, however please read special instructions on transporting number ranges**

Use

You must define number ranges for all of the corresponding business objects and document types in the EBP system. Number ranges will need to be maintained in EBP and SAP R/3 for:

- Shopping Carts
- Purchase Orders
- Goods Receipt (Confirmations)

Note: Any master data records replicated from R/3 to EBP will use the standard R/3 numbering assignment. For example, if a vendor number in R/3 is ABCCOMP, the vendor number in EBP for that vendor will be ABCCOMP as well.

*You can transport number range objects as follows:

a) On the Number Range screen, choose *Interval -> Transport*.
b) Make sure that at first all intervals of the number range object selected are deleted in the target system, so that only the exported intervals still exist after completion of the import. The current number levels are imported with the value that

they have at the time of export. Dependent tables are not transported or converted.

c) Alternatively, you can transport number ranges to all of your non-production systems, and then create them new in the production system during cutover to production.

Procedure

a.) Shopping Carts

SAP SRM Menu	*Supplier Relationship Management ? SRM Server ? Cross-Application Basic Settings ? Number Ranges ? SRM Server Number Ranges ? Define Number Ranges for Shopping Carts and Follow-on Documents*
Transa ction code	SPRO

Setting:

a) Click on the 'Change Intervals' button
b) Click on 'Insert Interval' and make the following entries. **NOTE: If the entry already exists, please just verify that the setting is correct.**

No.	From number	To number	External
10	1000000000	1999999999	

c) Click 'Save'.

b.) Purchase Orders

SAP SRM Menu	*Supplier Relationship Management ? SRM Server ? Cross-Application Basic Settings ? Number Ranges ? SRM Server Number Ranges ? Define Number Ranges for Local Purchase Orders*

Transaction code	SPRO

Setting:

a) Click on the 'Change Intervals' button
b) Click on 'Insert Interval' and make the following entries. **NOTE: If the entry already exists, please just verify that the setting is correct.**

No.	From number	To number	External
30	3000000000	3999999999	
70	7000000000	7999999999	

30 – Standard Purchase Orders
70 – Blanket Purchase Orders

c) Click 'Save'.

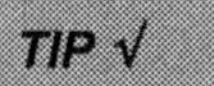

Since EBP purchase orders will be replicated to the R/3 system as read-only copies, the number range and document types for the purchase orders in EBP must be matched up with the number range and document types for the R/3 replicated purchase orders. Please reference the next section '5.2 Define Transaction Types in EBP' and '5.3 Define Transaction Types in R/3' for the configuration activities that need be completed in the EBP and R/3 application.

c.) Goods Receipts/Confirmations

SAP SRM Menu	*Supplier Relationship Management ? SRM Server ? Cross-Application Basic Settings ? Number Ranges ? SRM Server Number Ranges ? Define Number Ranges for Local Confirmations of Services and Goods Receipts*

Transaction code	SPRO

Setting:

a) Click on the 'Change Intervals' button
b) Click on 'Insert Interval' and make the following entries. **NOTE: If the entry already exists, please just verify that the setting is correct.**

No.	From number	To number	External
50	5000000000	5999999999	

c) Click 'Save'.

5.2) Define Transaction Types in EBP

Team Responsible:	**Functional Configuration**
Transportable:	**Yes**

Use

You must assign the number ranges previously defined to the document types for the following business objects.

- Shopping Carts
- Purchase Orders
- Goods Receipt (Confirmations)

Procedure

SAP SRM Menu	*Supplier Relationship Management ? SRM Server ? Cross-Application Basic Settings ? Define Transaction Types*

Transaction code	SPRO

Settings:
a.) SHOPPING CART

1.) Highlight the row with business object BUS2121 (Shopping Cart).
2.) Double click on 'Transaction Types' folder
3.) Enter the number range code previously defined in the 'Define Number Ranges' transaction for shopping carts in the 'Int. Number Range' field. ***Do not change the other default field values.***

TransactionType SHC

General

Description	Shopping Cart
Int. Number Range	10
Ext. Number Range	02
Status profile	
Trans. Cat.	BUS2121
Description	Shopping Cart

☐ Inactive

b.) PURCHASE ORDERS

DIRECT MATERIAL PURCHASE ORDERS (Only to be used for Plan-Driven Procurement scenarios)

1.) Highlight the row with business object BUS2201 (Purchase Order).
2.) Double click on 'Transaction Types' folder
3.) Double click on the row with the transaction type 'ECDP' (Direct Material Purchase Order)

4.) Select the 'Inactive' checkbox for this transaction.
5.) Click the 'Back' icon.

STANDARD PURCHASE ORDERS

1.) Double click on the row with the transaction type 'ECPO' (Purchase Order).
2.) Enter the number range code previously defined in the 'Define Number Ranges' transaction for purchase orders in the 'Int. Number Range' field. In this example, the number range is '30'
3.) In the 'Ext Number Range' field, enter the number range code '30' which will be defined later in the R/3 system.
4.) Click the 'Back' icon.

BLANKET PURCHASE ORDERS

1.) Since there is not a separate document type for Blanket Purchase Orders, we will create a new entry for blankets. To do this, click 'New Entries' in the 'Transaction Types' screen for the purchase order business object.
2.) Enter the following data:
    a. Transaction Type: ZBPO
    b. Description: Blanket Purch Order
    c. Int No. Range: 70
    d. Ext No Range: 70
    e. Status Profile: *Leave Blank*
    f. Trans. Cat: BUS2201
    g. Description: Blanket Purch Order
3.) Click the 'Back' icon

Click 'Save' to save all the work in a transport.

c.) GOODS RECEIPTS/CONFIRMATIONS

1.) Highlight the row with business object BUS2203 (Confirmations).
2.) Double click on 'Transaction Types' folder
3.) Enter the number range code previously defined in the 'Define Number Ranges' transaction for

goods receipts/confirmations in the 'Int. Number Range' field. ***Do not change the other default field values.***

5.3) R/3 Specific Configuration for Number Ranges and Document Types

Team Responsible:	**Functional Configuration**
Transportable:	**Yes**

Use
You must assign the corresponding number ranges in the R/3 system for the EBP purchase order document types and define the document types in R/3 for the EBP purchase orders.

A.) Number Ranges

Procedure

SAP R/3 Menu	*SAP Customizing Implementation Guide ? Materials Management ? Purchasing ? Purchase Order ? Define Number Ranges*
Transaction code	SPRO

Setting:

a.) Click on the 'Change Intervals' button
b.) Click on 'Insert Interval' and make the following entries.

No.	From number	To number	External
30	3000000000	3999999999	X
70	7000000000	7999999999	X

c.) Click 'Save'

B.) Document Types

Procedure

SAP R/3 Menu	*SAP Customizing Implementation Guide ? Materials Management ? Purchasing ? Purchase Order ? Define Document Types*
Transaction code	SPRO

Setting:

a.) Click on the 'New Entries' button on the menu bar
b.) Please make the following entries:
   a. Type: ECPO
   b. Doc. Type Description: EBP Purchase Order
   c. Item: 10
   d. No. Range Ext: 30
   e. Update Group: SAP
   f. Field Selection: NBF
c.) Highlight this new entry and double click the 'Allowed Item Categories' folder. Click on 'New Entries' and make the following settings:
   a. Standard
   b. Limit
d.) Click 'Back' and 'Save' (Note: You are not required to create any entries in the 'Link to Purchase Requisitions' folder).

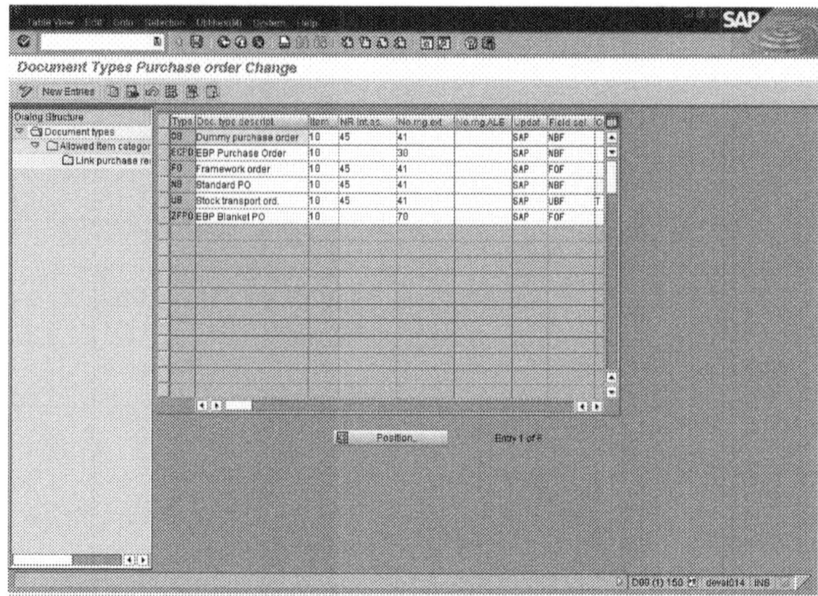

e.) Repeat steps a. – e. for the Blanket Purchase Order Doc Type. In step b.), please make the following settings:
   a. Type: ZBPO
   b. Doc. Type Description: EBP Blanket PO
   c. Item: 10
   d. No. Range Ext: 70
   e. Update Group: SAP
   f. Field Selection: FOF

f.) In Step c.), highlight the new entry and double click the 'Allowed Item Categories' folder. Click on 'New Entries' and make the following settings:
   a. Standard
   b. Limit
   c. Service (*Optional*)

6.) Master Data Replication

Team Responsible:	**Functional Configuration**
Transportable:	**No**

Use

The following master data objects will be replicated from R/3 to EBP. Any changes to these records will be done directly in the R/3 system and then updated into EBP.

- Units of Measure, Dimensions, and Currencies
- Material Groups (Product Categories in EBP)
- Material Master Records (Product Masters in EBP)
- Vendor Master Records ***(to be discussed in Section 10)***

Prerequisites

1.) Security Team needs to set up a User ID in R/3 for RFC calls from EBP to R/3 for replication. (Example: SRMRFCUSR)
2.) Validate that the load objects are maintained correctly

a) Access the transaction using:

SAP SRM Menu	*SAP R/3 to SAP SRM -> Customizing Replication -> Download Customizing Objects*
Transaction code	R3AC3

b) Switch to the change mode.

c) Activate only the following objects by setting NO flag in the Inactive column. Set the flag for all other objects.

- DNL_CUST_BASIS3
- DNL_CUST_PROD0
- DNL_CUST_PROD1
- DNL_CUST_SRVMAS

d) To replicate the active items in the back-end system, choose Save
e) Confirm message.

This process will need to be performed each time a new customizing object gets created in R/3.

Procedure

6.1) Replicate Units of Measure, Material Numbers, and Material Groups from R/3 to EBP

Step 1: Start Initial Load

SAP SRM Menu	N/A
Transaction code	R3AS

1.) Load Object: DNL_CUST_BASIS3 - For new units of measure, dimensions and currencies
2.) Click the "Execute" icon to begin the replication process.

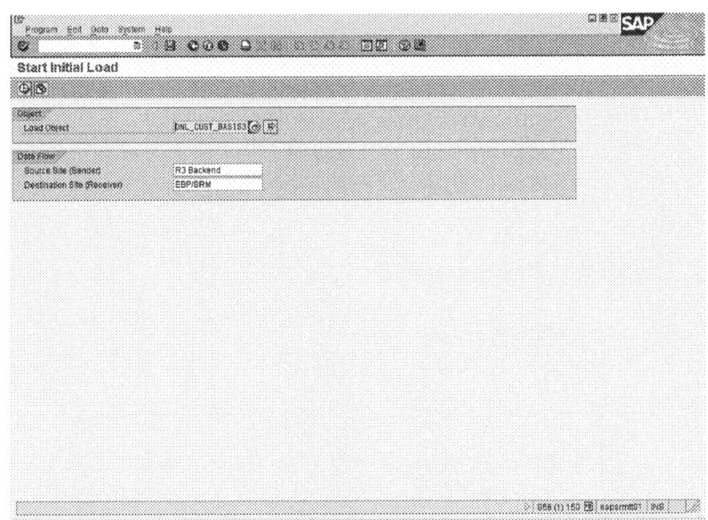

3.) If the job has been successfully initiated, you should receive a message like the one in the screenshot below.

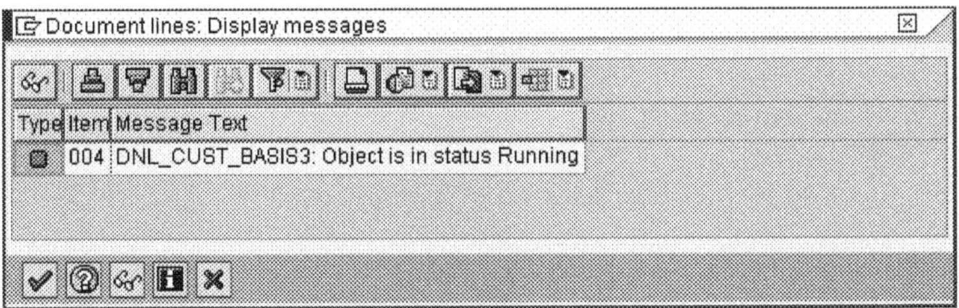

4.) Repeat steps 1-3 for the following objects after the DNL_CUST_BASIS3 has been executed successfully (execute the load objects in the following sequence):

- DNL_CUST_PROD0 – For new material masters (product masters in EBP)
- DNL_CUST_PROD1 – For new material groups (product category in EBP)

Note: *DNL_CUST_SRVMAS – New service masters (service categories in EBP) –***If Service Masters are in scope for the EBP implementation, replicate the service master sheets into EBP from R/3.***

Step 2: View the status of the replication

SAP SRM Menu	N/A
Transaction code	R3AM1

1.) Enter the object name of the replication you wish to monitor (i.e. DNL_CUST_BASIS3) and then click the 'Execute' icon.

R3AM1 – View status of replication

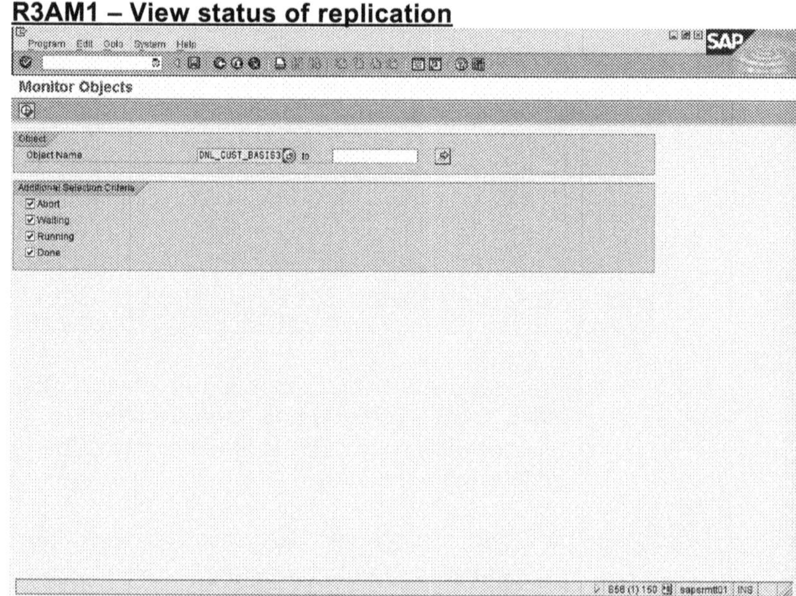

2.) The screen below notes that the replication is running (yellow light). This will turn green which the replication has successfully been completed.

Click the Refresh icon 

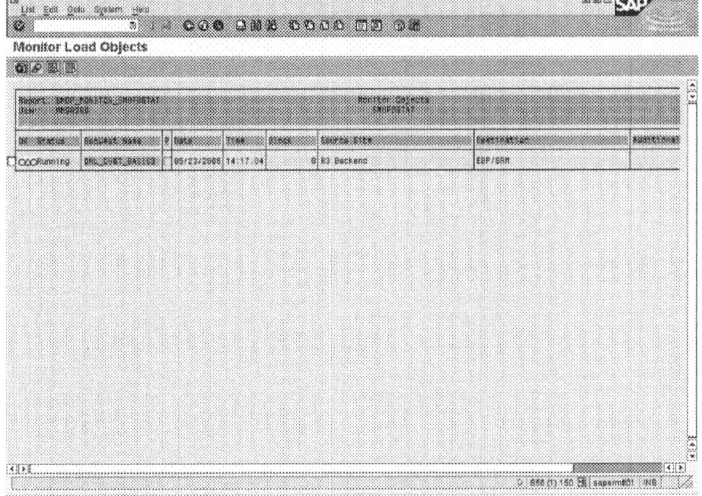

3.) If the load has successfully completed, the 'Status' column should have a green light and the status should be set to 'Done'. If the status is still 'yellow' or 'red', please reference the 'Tip' **Troubleshooting Object Replication from R/3 to EBP** below.

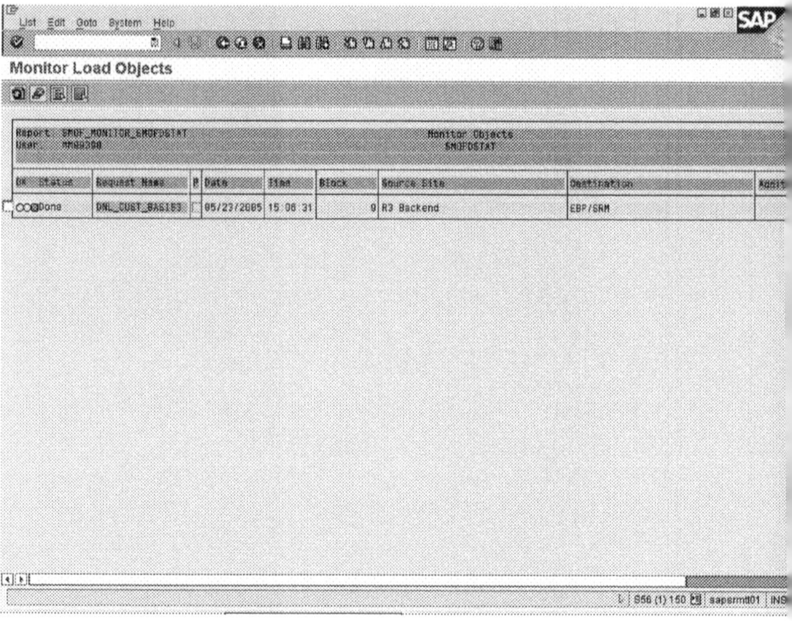

4.) Repeat Steps 1 and 2 for the following load objects:
    - DNL_CUST_PROD0 – For new material master types (product masters in EBP)
    - DNL_CUST_PROD1 – For new material groups (product category in EBP)

5.) Once the loads have completed, execute transaction **COMM_HIERARCHY** in EBP to check whether the material types and groups have been replicated into the EBP system.

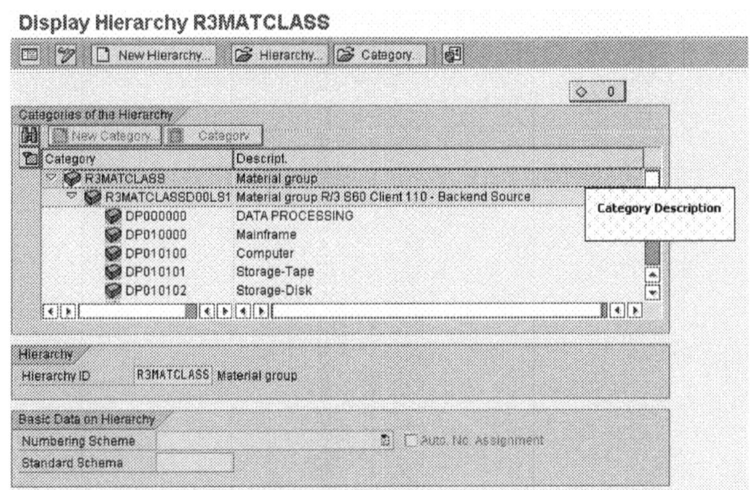

TIP √ **Troubleshooting Object Replication from R/3 to EBP**

Occasionally, the replication objects get stuck in the R/3 queue and are not replicated to the EBP backend system. You can check the status of any replication job by executing transaction R3AM1. If the job has been running for a long time and has not completed, please reference the following steps.

1. Execute transaction code SMQ1 in the R/3 backend to check the data replication queue in the R/3 backend system.

SMQ1 in SAP R/3

2. To check the queue in EBP, use transaction SMQ2. Then click "Execute".

SMQ2 in EBP

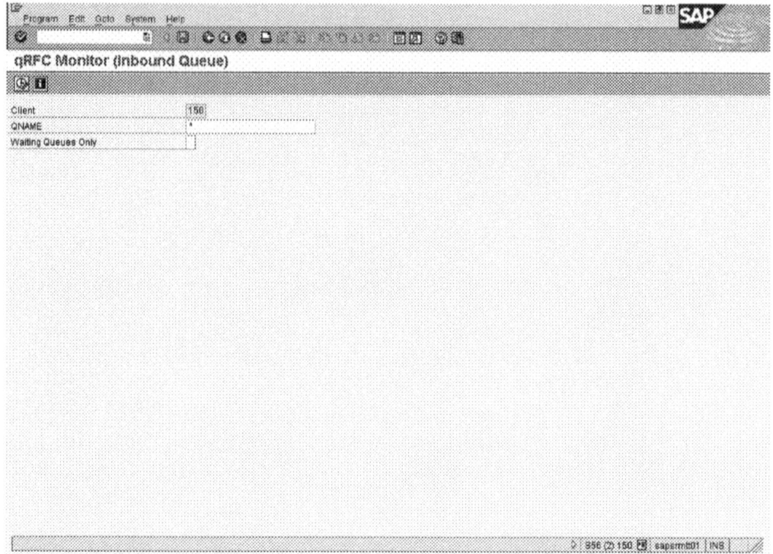

3. Choose the job you wish to monitor and click "Display"

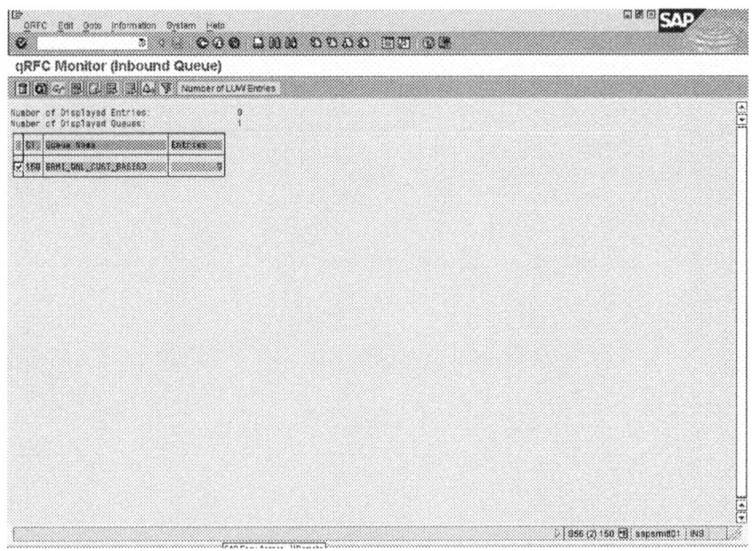

4. If you login and see that status is READY then double click on the entry and activate using this activate icon and the Status will change to Running.

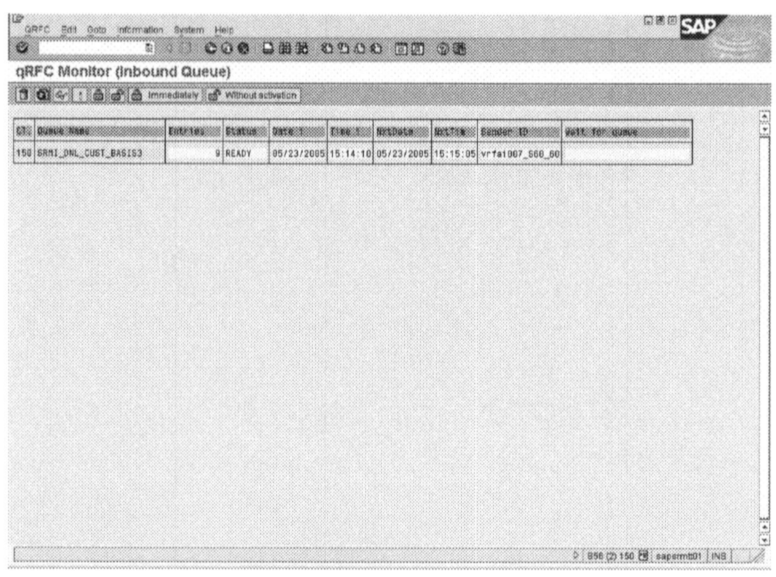

6.2) Validate Units of Measure, Currencies, and Exchange Rates

Team Responsible:	**Basis – Setup** **Functional Configuration - Validation**
Transportable:	**No**

Use
Validate that the units of measure, currencies, and exchange rates in the *SAP Enterprise Buyer* system corresponds to those in the backend system.

Procedure

Activity	Description	Further Information

Checking units of measurement	The contents of the Customizing table "Unit of measurement" must be identical in *SAP Enterprise Buyer* and in the backend system. **The UOM is replicated from R/3 to EBP via the data replication procedure DNL_CUST_BASIS3**	Path in the Implementation Guide (IMG): *SAP Web Application Server* ? *General Settings* ? *Check Units of Measurement* *Transaction Code: CUNI* The measurements in EBP should be consistent with the units of measurement being used in PO Generator. Be sure to replicate units of measurement, which were added to the delivered options in PO Generator. Note: The delivered replication method will also update the corresponding ISO code.
Aligning	To align the currencies	**See section 2.1**

currencies and exchange rates	and exchange rates in the backend system with those in *SAP Enterprise Buyer*, run the reports BBP_GET_CURRENCY and BBP_GET_EXRATE whenever currencies and exchange rates are updated in the backend system.	**'Scheduling Reports'**
Allocating ISO codes	Allocate the relevant ISO codes, in particular if you are connecting to catalogs.	Path in the Implementation Guide (IMG): *SAP Web Application Server* ? *General Settings* ? *Check Units of Measurement* *Settings: Click the 'ISO Codes' button and verify if there is a list of ISO codes maintained in the table.*

6.3) Material Master Replication

Team Responsible:	**Functional Configuration**

Transportable:	**No**

Use

Material master records created in R/3 can be replicated to the EBP system and then made available in the CCM catalog for EBP Requestors to shop from. In order to bring over material master records which contain purchasing data, we will set filters in EBP using transaction R3AC1.

Procedure

Step 1: Setting Filters on Material Masters

SAP SRM Menu	N/A
Transaction code	R3AC1

EBP provides standard functionality for filtering which material masters are replicated from R/3 to EBP. This is done using Transaction **R3AC1.** Below are the 5 material master tables that can be used to filter. Fields in each of these tables can also be used to refine the filter.

R3AC1 – Set Filters

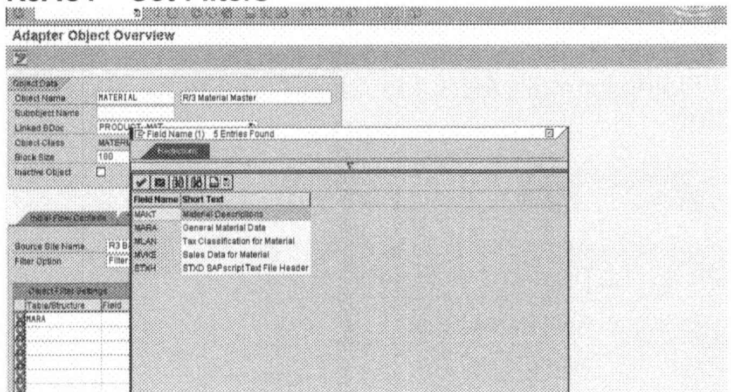

A.) Field from the MAKT – Material Description table

Table Name	Field Name	Short T...
MAKT	SPRAS	

B.) Fields from MARA – General Material data table

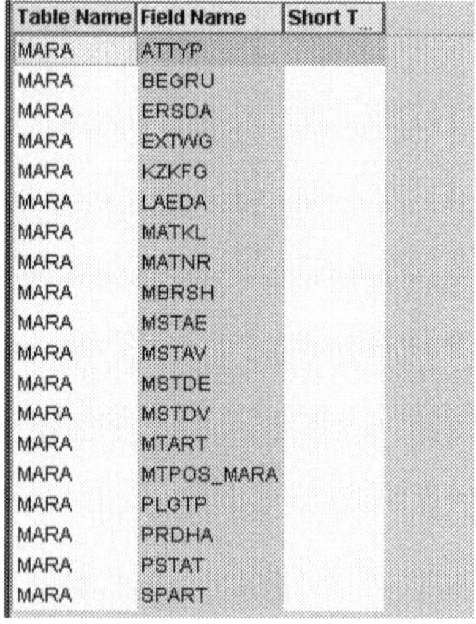

Table Name	Field Name	Short T...
MARA	ATTYP	
MARA	BEGRU	
MARA	ERSDA	
MARA	EXTWG	
MARA	KZKFG	
MARA	LAEDA	
MARA	MATKL	
MARA	MATNR	
MARA	MBRSH	
MARA	MSTAE	
MARA	MSTAV	
MARA	MSTDE	
MARA	MSTDV	
MARA	MTART	
MARA	MTPOS_MARA	
MARA	PLGTP	
MARA	PRDHA	
MARA	PSTAT	
MARA	SPART	

C.) Fields from MLAN – Tax Classification for Material table

Table Name	Field Name	Short T...
MLAN	ALAND	

D.) Fields from Sales for Material table

MVKE	BONUS
MVKE	DWERK
MVKE	KONDM
MVKE	KTGRM
MVKE	MATKC
MVKE	MTPOS
MVKE	MVGR1
MVKE	MVGR2
MVKE	MVGR3
MVKE	MVGR4
MVKE	MVGR5
MVKE	PMATN
MVKE	PRAT1
MVKE	PRAT2
MVKE	PRAT3
MVKE	PRAT4
MVKE	PRAT5
MVKE	PRAT6
MVKE	PRAT7
MVKE	PRAT8
MVKE	PRAT9
MVKE	PRATA
MVKE	PRODH
MVKE	PROVG
MVKE	VKORG
MVKE	VMSTA
MVKE	VMSTD
MVKE	VTWEG

Configuration Activity

Relevant OSS Notes: 519794

Set a filter to only replicate materials with a purchasing view by maintaining a filter for the 'Maintenance Status' field PSTAT for material master records. This filter will look for any value of 'E' (Purchasing View) in the 'Maintenance Status' field and replicate only those records with a value of at least 'E' in the field.

1. Start Transaction R3AC1
2. Go to the maintenance of object MATERIAL.
3. Go to the filter settings title element and select the system(s) for replication.
4. For each system create a filter entry with the following values:
   Tab: MARA
   Field: PSTAT
   OP: Contains Pattern
   Low: *E* (The letter 'E' means that there is a purchasing view maintained for the material master record)
   High: (SPACE)
   Incl.Excl: Inclusive

Other filters will possibly be used to exclude material master records, which have been blocked for purchasing across all plants and/or material master records that are flagged for deletion. For example, the field used for determining if a material is blocked in a plant/s is:

Table: MARA
Field: MSTAE – Cross-plant material status

Step 2: Start Initial Load for Material Master Records

SAP SRM Menu	FILL IN
Transaction code	R3AS

1.) Load Object: MATERIAL - For material master records
2.) Click the "Execute" icon to begin the replication process.

This data replication procedure can be monitored using the previously mentioned transactions. **This may also be set up as a batch process.**

R3AS – Start Initial Load

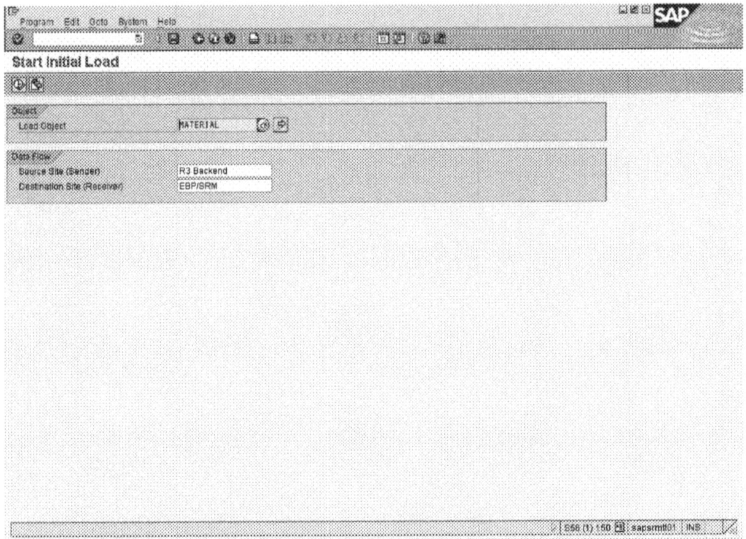

3.) After the report has executed, execute transaction COMMPR01 to see the product master records that have been replicated from R/3 to EBP.

Transaction Code: COMMPR01 – Maintain Products

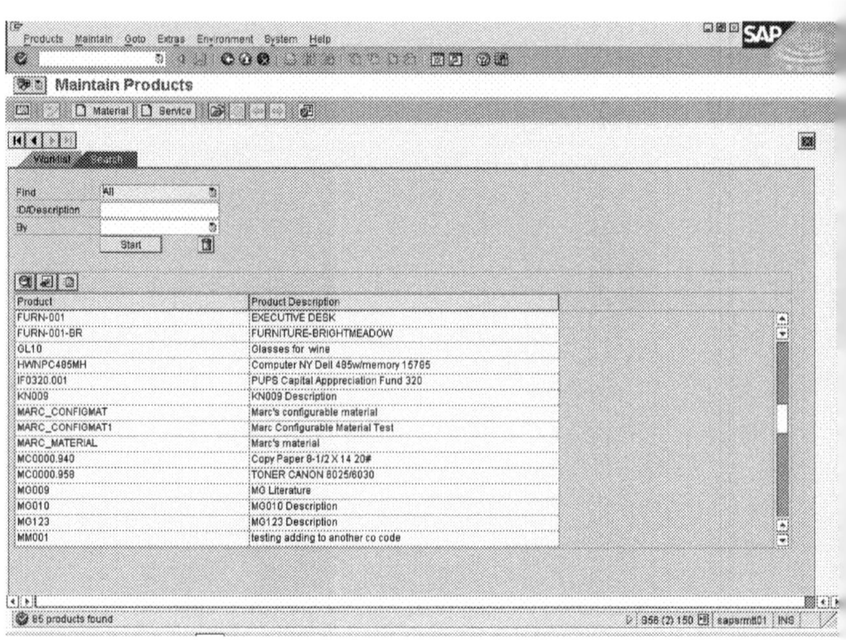

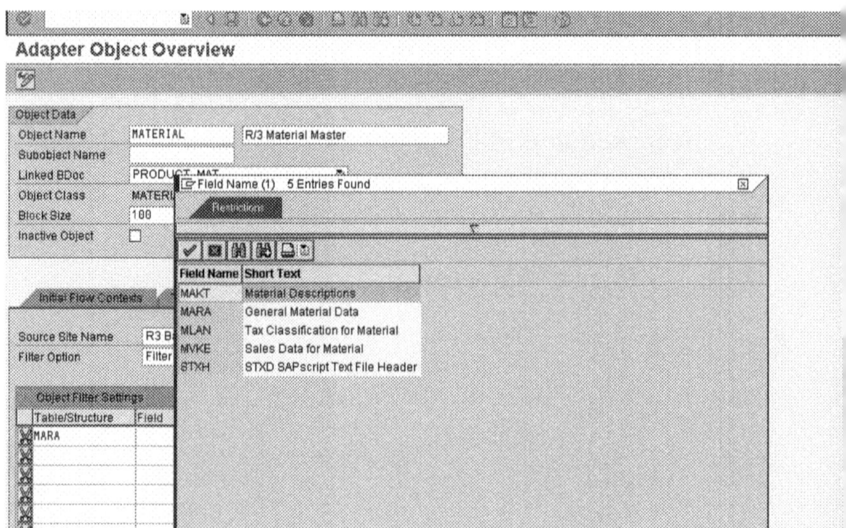

7.) Make Settings for Locations and External Business Partners

Team Responsible:	**Functional Configuration**
Transportable:	**Not Transportable**

Use
This section describes the settings you need to make for locations and external business partners.

Prerequisites

You have completed the following steps:

- Define business partner groupings and assigned number ranges

You must ensure that at least one standard grouping has been defined and that the standard indicator has been set for external number assignment. See the SAP Implementation Guide under *Cross-Application Components ? SAP Business Partner ? Business Partner ? Basic Settings ? Number Ranges and Groupings ? Define Groupings and Assign Number Ranges*.

Setting: Leave the default settings

- Define number ranges for address management

See the SAP Implementation Guide under *SAP Web Application Server ? Web Application Server ? Basis Services ? Address Management ? Maintain Address and Person Number Range (Transaction Code: SA01)*

Setting: Leave the default settings

- Define partner functions

You can enter the texts you want to use for the partner function for a partner function type. These texts are displayed in the relevant documents for a business transaction. See the SAP Implementation Guide *SRM Server ? Cross-Application Basic Settings ? Define Partner Functions*

Setting: Validate that Partner Function 'Location' exists in the table.

- Execute report BBP_ATTR_XPRA400 via SE38 in the EBP system. This report will prepare all of the system parameters for the replication of locations.

7.1) Replicate Plants

Procedure

SRM Menu	*N/A*
Transaction code	SE38

1.) There are three reports that can be executed to replicate plants from the backend system and store them as business partners in EBP. They are:

Report Name	**Report Description**
BBP_LOCATIONS_GET_ALL	Gets all the location numbers from each backend

	system that is connected.
BBP_LOCATIONS_GET_SELECTED	Gets selected locations
BBP_LOCATIONS_GET_FROM_SYSTEM	Gets all the location numbers from one particular backend system.

2.) Use report BBP_LOCATIONS_GET_ALL* to replicate all plants from the backend system to EBP.
3.) Click 'Execute' to begin the report.

**** Using BBP_LOCATIONS_GET_SELECTED - When replicating plants for the first time, please use the report BBP_LOCATIONS_GET_ALL. If you need to update new plants added to the system, you can utilize report BBP_LOCATIONS_GET_SELECTED to replicate specific plants from R/3 to EBP***

1.) Enter the backend system in the 'Logical System' field
2.) In the 'Data Transfer for Plant(s)' field, enter plant '1100' and then click the 'Multiple Selection' icon, enter all of the plant numbers that you want to replicate and click the 'Copy' icon.
3.) Click 'Execute' to begin the report

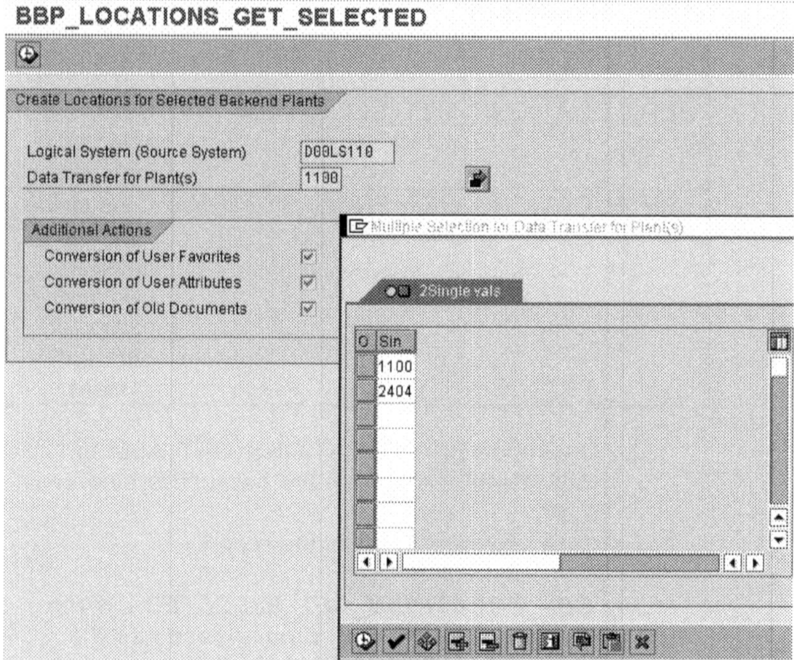

7.2) Verify Settings for External Business Partners

Prerequisites

- You must first create the organizational plan with at least one organizational unit to which the external business partners can be assigned (vendor root node). ***See Section 2.11***

- You must create Business Number Ranges and Groupings. Note: *The Internal Business Number Range should NOT conflict with the External Number Range for Vendors.*

  1.) Define Number Ranges

SAP SRM IMG Menu	*Cross-Application Components ? SAP Business Partner ? Business Partner ? Basic Settings ? Number Ranges and Groupings ? Define Number Ranges.*
Transaction code	SPRO

Setting: Deselect the 'External' flag for the MD number range. This is to prevent any confusion in the EBP system when assigning a number range to vendors replicated from the backend system.

2.) Define Groupings and Assign Number Ranges

SAP SRM IMG Menu	*Cross-Application Components ? SAP Business Partner ? Business Partner ? Basic Settings ? Number Ranges and Groupings ? Define Groupings and Assign Number Ranges.*
Transaction code	SPRO

When replicating vendors from multiple backend systems, the number range for which the standard indicator has been set is used for external number assignment. Therefore, it is recommended that this number range is great enough to cover all number ranges set in the individual backend systems.

Setting: Leave default settings

Procedure

Replicate the vendor business partner records as described in Section 7.3 below.

7.3) Replicate Vendor Master Records

Team Responsible:	**Functional Configuration**
Transportable:	**No**

Use

This section describes replicating vendor master records from the R/3 backend to EBP. When vendors are replicated, a business partner number is generated in EBP. Since vendor master records are maintained with external numbering assignment in the R/3 backend, the business partner number for vendors in EBP will exactly match the external numbering scheme in R/3.

Prerequisites

- Verify all the settings are made in Section 7.2
- Create root organizational unit for vendor records in the EBP Org. Structure (example: VNDR_ROOT) as discussed in Section 2.9
- (*Optional*) Incoterms (both the code and description) are maintained in the Vendor Master Record Purchasing view in the R/3 system (this is only required if incoterms are required fields in the R/3 Purchase Order)
- Execute program BBP_UPLOAD_PAYMENT_TERMS via transaction code SE38 to replicate all of the existing payment terms from the backend to EBP.
- (*Optional*) – Communication method is maintained for all vendors if the preferred transmission medium method is E-Mail or Fax.

Important OSS Notes:
859898 – BBPGETVD: Total number of vendors to be replicated incorrectly

Procedure

A.) Creating Vendor Master Records

SAP Program	BBP_VENDOR_GET_DATA
Transaction code	SE38

Setting:

1.) Enter program name 'BBP_VENDOR_GET_DATA' and click 'Execute' (alternatively, you can enter transaction code BBPGETVD in the transaction code menu – can not be called directly in the SAP Easy Access menu)
2.) Enter the following values:
   a. Source System: Select the system ID of the backend system
   b. Purchasing Organization: Enter the purchasing organization (example: POG1)
   c. Verify the 'Address Comparison to Identify Duplicates' checkbox is selected.
   d. In the 'Object ID' under Organizational Unit for Vendor, enter the vendor root organizational unit node.
   e. Select the radio button 'Only Transfer R/3 numbers' as the vendor master records in R/3 use external number assignment.
3.) Click 'Start Transfer' button at bottom of the screen.

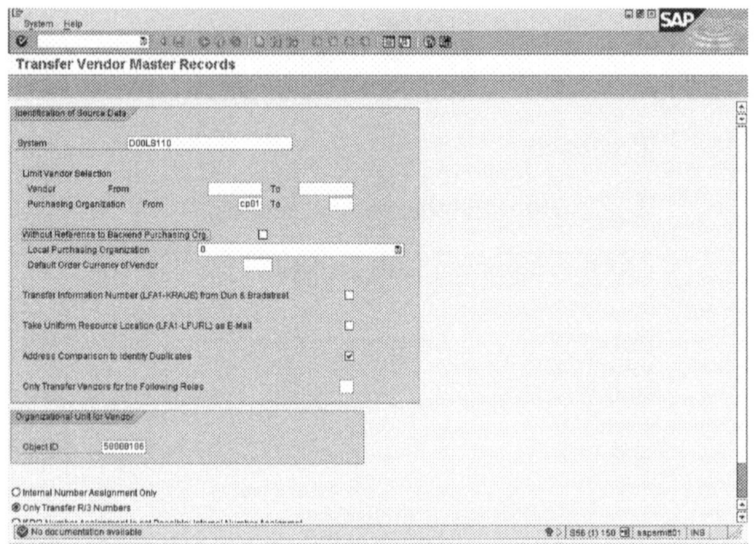

4.) In the subsequent screen, review the list of proposed vendors that will be replicated from the backend system and click 'Start Transmission'. NOTE: A warning message could appear with a list of vendors that cannot be replicated due to external number assignment.

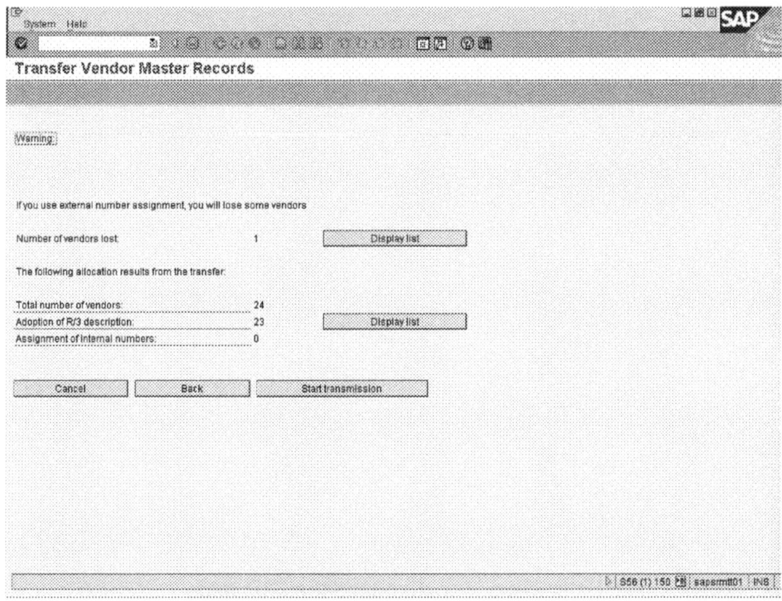

5.) A pop-up message will appear stating the replication process has started.

6.) To view the application log for the vendor replication job, execute transaction code SLG1. In the 'Business Object' field, enter the object name 'BBPGETVD' and click 'Execute'. Review the log to verify if the vendors were replicated correctly or if there is any warning or error messages generated during the job.

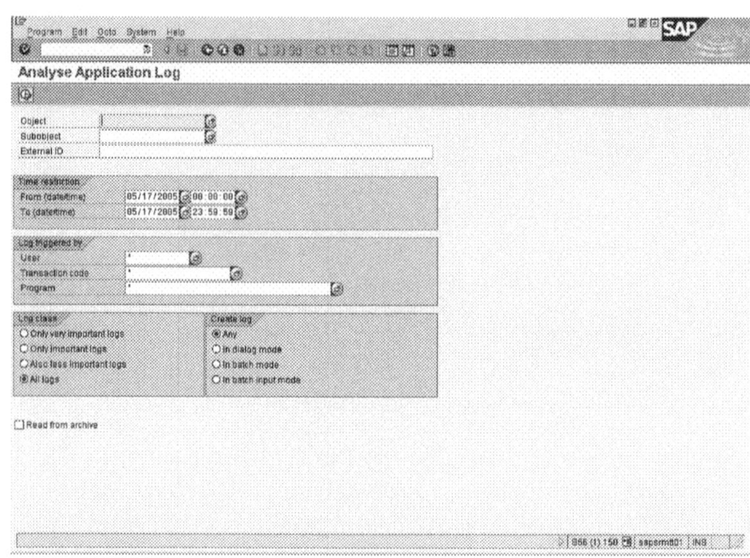

B.) Updating Vendor Master Records

SRM Menu	N/A
Transaction code	BBPUPDVD (can not be called via the SAP Easy Access Menu)

Setting:

1.) Enter transaction code BBPUPDVD in the transaction code menu – can not be called directly in the SAP Easy Access menu)

2.) Enter the following values:
   a. Source System: Select the system ID of the backend system
   b. Purchasing Organization: Enter the purchasing organization (example: POG1)
   c. Select the checkbox 'Without reference to Backend Purchasing Organization'

d. Select the 'Suppression of Change Documents' checkbox to stop change documents to be written to the database during the vendor update replication.

3.) Click 'Start Transfer' button at bottom of the screen.
4.) In the subsequent screen, review the list of proposed vendors that will be updated from the backend system and click 'Start Update'.

Scheduling Vendor Update Job

Step 1: Make configuration settings for automated vendor synchronization:

SRM IMG Menu	*Supplier Relationship Management → SRM Server → Technical Basic Settings → Settings for Vendor Synchronization → Make Global Settings*
Transaction code	SPRO

1.) Click 'New Entries'
2.) Make the following settings as depicted in the screenshot below.

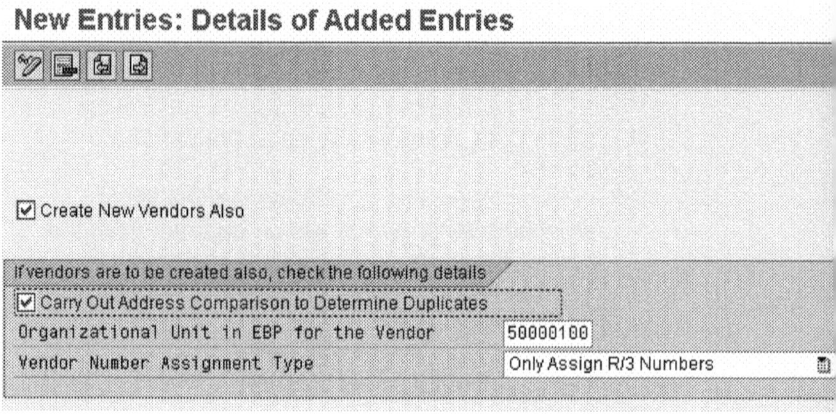

New Entries: Details of Added Entries

☑ Create New Vendors Also

If vendors are to be created also, check the following details

☑ Carry Out Address Comparison to Determine Duplicates

Organizational Unit in EBP for the Vendor 50000100

Vendor Number Assignment Type Only Assign R/3 Numbers

Step 2: Make configuration settings for automated vendor synchronization:

SRM IMG Menu	*Supplier Relationship Management → SRM Server → Technical Basic Settings → Settings for Vendor Synchronization → Define Settings for Each Backend System*
Transaction code	SPRO

1.) Click ‘New Entries’
2.) Make the following entries:
    a. Order: Select ‘0001’ from the drop down
    b. Logical System: Select the corresponding backend system from the drop down
    c. Select the ‘NoEBP Purchasing Org’ checkbox
    d. Click ‘Save’

Step 3: Create variant for BBP_VENDOR_SYNC report

SRM IMG Menu	N/A
Transaction code	SA38

1.) Enter 'BBP_VENDOR_SYNC' in the report field
2.) Click on the pushbutton *Background*.
3.) Create a new variant for the report by selecting the 'Variant'. Enter the variant name such as ZVENDOR_SYNC and click the 'Create' button next to variant name
4.) For the report variant, verify that the 'From last update' radio button is selected (no other changes are required).
5.) Click the 'Attributes' button and enter a short description in the 'Meaning' field for the variant.
6.) Click 'Save'

Step 4: Schedule BBP_VENDOR_SYNC report*

***This task should be completed by the BASIS team.**

SRM IMG Menu	N/A
Transaction code	SA38

1.) Enter the variant for the 'BBP_VENDOR_SYNC' in the report field
2.) Click on the pushbutton *Schedule*
3.) Enter Job Name and click 'Schedule Periodically'
4.) Define the period interval (example: Every 2 minutes)
5.) Click 'Save'

NOTE √

Note: The BBP_VENDOR_SYNC program does not pick up the communication methods defined in the vendor master record in the backend while the regular vendor update program BBP_VENDOR_UPDATE_DATA_JOB does pick up the communication method. Therefore, if you want to pick up communication methods, it is recommended that you schedule the report BBP_VENDOR_UPDATE_DATA_JOB to execute upon completion of the BBP_VENDOR_SYNC job.

8.) EBP Organizational Structure and Attributes

8.1) Create Organizational Structure

Team Responsible:	**Functional Configuration**
Transportable:	**Not transportable through SAP transports, but possible via ALE**

Use
The EBP organizational structure is a fundamental requirement in order for the EBP system to function. It contains all of the Parameter IDs and relationship rules to allow Shopping Cart Creators, Buyers, Approvers, and Goods Recipients to use and interact with the EBP system.

Prerequisites

- The Root Organizational Unit and corresponding purchasing organization (listed under the root) has been created in EBP as identified in Section 2.10

- Make settings for HR Integration with Organizational Management

SAP SRM IMG Menu	*Supplier Relationship Management ? SRM Server ? Cross-Application Basic Settings ? Organizational Management ? Integration Business Partners-Organizational Management ? Set Up Integration with Organizational Management*

Transaction code	SPRO

Setting: These settings need only be established in the initial configuration of an SRM client. Validate that there is a 'X' in the HRAC parameter to allow proper transfer of address changes in the organizational structure with any business partner records.

Validate the other entries as listed in the screenshot below.

Change View "HR: Set Up Central Person": Overview

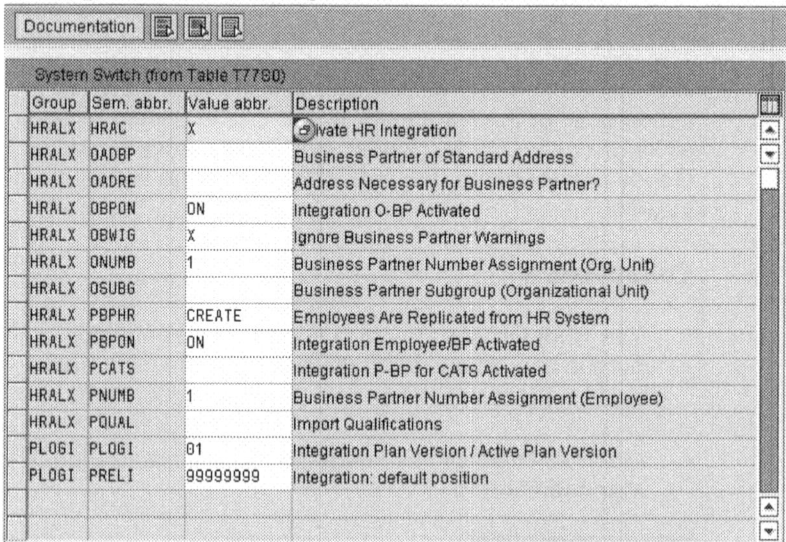

Documentation

System Switch (from Table T77S0)

Group	Sem. abbr.	Value abbr.	Description
HRALX	HRAC	X	ivate HR Integration
HRALX	OADBP		Business Partner of Standard Address
HRALX	OADRE		Address Necessary for Business Partner?
HRALX	OBPON	ON	Integration O-BP Activated
HRALX	OBWIG	X	Ignore Business Partner Warnings
HRALX	ONUMB	1	Business Partner Number Assignment (Org. Unit)
HRALX	OSUBG		Business Partner Subgroup (Organizational Unit)
HRALX	PBPHR	CREATE	Employees Are Replicated from HR System
HRALX	PBPON	ON	Integration Employee/BP Activated
HRALX	PCATS		Integration P-BP for CATS Activated
HRALX	PNUMB	1	Business Partner Number Assignment (Employee)
HRALX	PQUAL		Import Qualifications
PLOGI	PLOGI	01	Integration Plan Version / Active Plan Version
PLOGI	PRELI	99999999	Integration: default position

Description of each entry

1. **Integration activation:** The integration must be activated with the main switch (HRALX/ HRAC = X, previously CPERS/ EEALE).

2. **Organizational unit integration:** To activate the integration between business partners and organizational units, switch HRALX/ OBPON=ON (previously BUPA/ SYNC) must be set.
3. **Employee integration:** To activate the integration between business partners and employees, switch HRALX/ PBPON=ON must be set.
4. **Roles:** For business partners in the role *organizational unit* the role description is maintained in HRALX/OPROL=BUP004 (previously ORGEH/ PROLE); for *employee* it is maintained in HRALX/PPROL=BUP003 (previously BUPA/ PROL). *Note: The values maintained here are used to create a business partner role when business partner master records are created from organizational units.*
5. **Number assignment:** Generally speaking, there are three ways of assigning numbers when generating business parters.

    a) As before, a number is taken from the general internal interval of the number range object BU_PARTNER.

    b) A number is taken from the special internal interval of the object.

    c) A number is adopted from HR and assigned a prefix. A special external interval is used for this, which must be defined between XX00000000 and XX99999999 (XX represent any two letters).

For organizational units, numbers are assigned with HRALX/ONUMB; for employees, numbers are assigned with HRALX/PNUMB.
The number range object for switch settings is BU_PARTNER and the interval is dependent on the switch value. For switch value 1, the internal interval is used. Otherwise (for switch values 2 and 3), the interval is defined by switches HRALX/OSUBG and HRALX/PSUNG. Additionally for switch values 2 and 3, a grouping must be created (transaction BUC2) for these intervals. So that the system can connect the

grouping and number range interval, the name of the grouping must be identical to the name of the corresponding number range interval (the name of the grouping is in the first column of the table). If you choose type 3 (switch HRALX/ PNUMB=3) for the number assignment of business partners of the employee role, please create switch HRALX/PSUBG manually in table T77S0.

6. **Error workflow:** If users should be informed of errors by e-mail, recipients can be defined in switch HRALX/ MSGRE (0=no messages, 1=workflow administrator is informed, 2=user receives e-mail, 3=both are informed).

7. **Addresses:** If addresses are required to correctly generate business partners, switch HRALX/OADRE=X is set (previously BUPA/ADDR). The standard address, which is assigned to every organizational unit without its own address, can be defined with HRALX/OADPB (previously BUPA/ADRBP). Here, a business partner is created with an address and his number is entered in the switch.

8. **Link to the user:** Usually, a link is created to the user (infotype 0105, subtype 0001) only if the user already exists in the target system. However, this can be changed using switch HRALX/ USRAC. If this switch is set to 'X', links are also created to users that do not exist in the system (see Note 711852).

See also:
Note 550055: EBP/CRM: New integration for business partner

Procedure

Step 1: Create additional organizational units for your respective company codes/divisions/departments

SAP SRM IMG Menu	*Supplier Relationship Management ? SRM Server ? Cross-Application Basic Settings ? Organizational Management ? Change Organizational Plan*
Transaction code	PPOMA_BBP

Settings:

1.) Enter the validity period as the current date and leave the valid to date as '12/31/9999'.
2.) In the 'Basic Data' tab for the new org unit enter the appropriate Short Description and Long Description for the Org Unit (For example: COR1 and Coporate Head Office)
3.) Click the 'Address' tab and enter a valid address for the root org. unit.
4.) Click the 'Function' tab. If the org unit is a company code, select the company code checkbox and enter the company code name and the corresponding backend system.
5.) Click Save.
6.) Repeat steps 1-5 for additional organizational units

Step 2: Create additional organizational units for purchasing groups

SAP SRM IMG Menu	*Supplier Relationship Management ? SRM Server ? Cross-Application Basic Settings ? Organizational Management ? Change Organizational Plan*
Transaction code	PPOMA_BBP

Settings:

1.) Enter the validity period as the current date and leave the valid to date as '12/31/9999'.
2.) In the 'Basic Data' tab for the new org unit enter the appropriate Short Description and Long Description for the Org Unit
3.) Click the 'Address' tab and enter a valid address for the root org. unit.
4.) Click the 'Function' tab. Select the 'Purchasing Group' checkbox and enter the purchasing group code from the backend in the 'Corresponds To' text field. Leave the source system field blank.

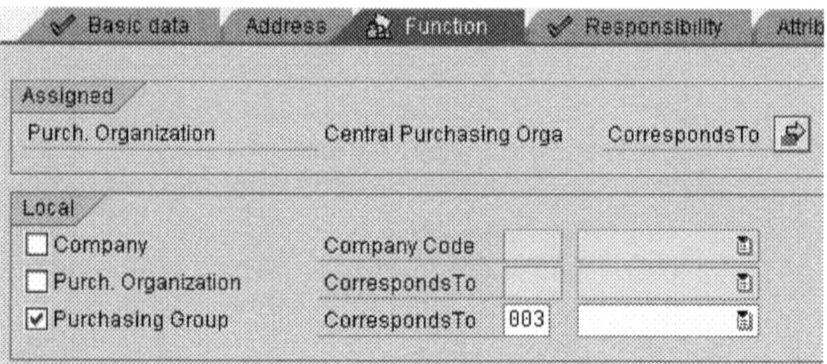

5.) Click Save.
6.) Repeat steps 1-5 for additional purchasing groups.

8.2) Maintain User Attributes

Team Responsible:	**Functional Configuration**
Transportable:	**Not transportable through SAP transports, but possible via ALE**

Use

Every org. unit and person in the EBP org. structure must be assigned attributes. Attributes in EBP are analogous to parameter Ids in SAP R/3 and include entries such as plant, company code, cost center, currency code, and catalogs. Attributes control the default settings and available selections for access when a user logs into the EBP system.

Prerequisites

- Organizational units have been created in the EBP organizational structure.

- Plants have been replicated from R/3 to EBP

Procedure

Step 1: Assign Enterprise-Level Attributes – These attributes will be entered at the root organizational unit (i.e., Corporate Enterprise) and will be inherited by all of the children organizational units and users.

SAP SRM IMG Menu	*Supplier Relationship Management ? SRM Server ? Cross-Application Basic Settings ? Organizational Management ? Change Organizational Plan*
Transaction code	PPOMA_BBP

Settings:

1.) Select the Root Organizational Unit and click on the 'Attributes' tab.
2.) Enter the following root org. unit attributes:

Attribute	Description and Example Value	Definition	Root Org. Unit Attribute

ACS	System alias for accounting systems Example value: D00CLNT100	Name of the backend system client (R/3) where the account assignment is validated.	X
BSA	Transaction type: Shopping cart follow-on document Example value: S00CLNT150\ECPO	Defines the transaction type in the respective system for follow-on documents from shopping carts. The attribute needs to be defined once per system, for the local SAP Enterprise Buyer System and for all connected backend systems.	X

BWA	Movement type Example value: D00CLNT100\201	Defines the type of goods movement in the backend system.	X
CUR	Local currency Example value: USD	Default currency of the user	X
FORWARD_WI	Flag: Forward work item Example value: X	Indicator: Specifies whether work items are to be forwarded as e-mails.	X
ITS_DEST	Current ITS of a user Example value: http://sapsrmuit:80/sap/bc/gui/its/webgui	Current address of the user's Internet access (supplied automatically)	X
KNT	Account assignment category Example value: CC	Default value for account assignment when creating shopping cart or lean purchase order.	X

		The default value for the account assignment is determined on the basis of the value for this attribute (for example CC – cost center) in connection with the relevant account assignment object (in this example CNT cost center). Note: In Customizing, no check occurs to establish whether the value for the relevant account assignment object is maintained.	

SYS	System alias Example value: D00CLNT100	Defines the systems(example: R/3) to be searched to find purchase orders. This attribute is used to generate worklists for employees that create confirmations or invoices centrally. The attribute can refer both to the local system and the backend system. Generally, several values are defined: The local systems and various backend systems.	X

TOG	Tolerance group Example value: CONF	Defines the tolerance group. Using this attribute, you define for a user group which tolerance checks are used when quantity or value tolerances for deliveries or invoices are exceeded.	**Optional at Root**
VENDOR _ACS	Accounting system for the vendor Example value: SAP R/3 Backend System ID	Specifies the backend system where the account assignment is checked. This attribute is required for: 3. Invoices without purchase order reference 4. Local invoices	X

VENDOR_SYS	System alias for vendor Example value: SAP R/3 Backend System ID	Defines the systems to be searched to find purchase orders to create a worklist for a vendor creating confirmations or invoices centrally. Can refer both to the local system and to the backend system. Generally, multiple values are entered: The local systems and various backend systems.	X

3.) Click the 'Save' icon in the EBP Org. Structure.

Screenshots of example high-level root org. unit attributes

A.) System Alias – This is the name of the backend system where the account assignment is checked. It is required for invoices without PO reference (in the case of a vendor, the backend system is determined using the attribute VENDOR_ACS).

Basic data | Attributes | Extended Attributes | Function

Description	Exclu	Default	Inherit	Attribute	Value
Commitment Item				ACC_CMITEM	
Funct. Area				ACC_FCAREA	
Funds Center				ACC_FCENTR	
Fund				ACC_FUND	
Grant				ACC_GRANT	
System Alias for Acc			✓	ACS	D00LS110

B.) Document type in R/3 system - This is the name of the follow-on document type for a Purchase Order that is used in R/3 - You must enter the system and then the document type.

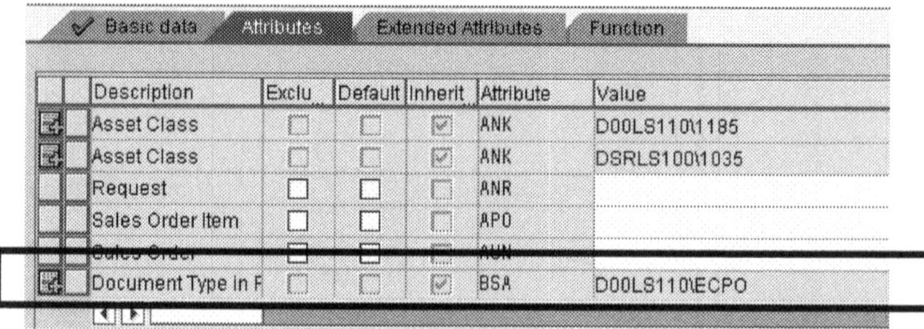
Basic data | Attributes | Extended Attributes | Function

Description	Exclu	Default	Inherit	Attribute	Value
Asset Class			✓	ANK	D00LS110\1185
Asset Class			✓	ANK	DSRLS100\1035
Request				ANR	
Sales Order Item				APO	
Sales Order				AUN	
Document Type in F			✓	BSA	D00LS110\ECPO

Local Currency – This is the local currency which the Shopping Cart creator will be ordering goods in (for example, USD, GBP, etc.)

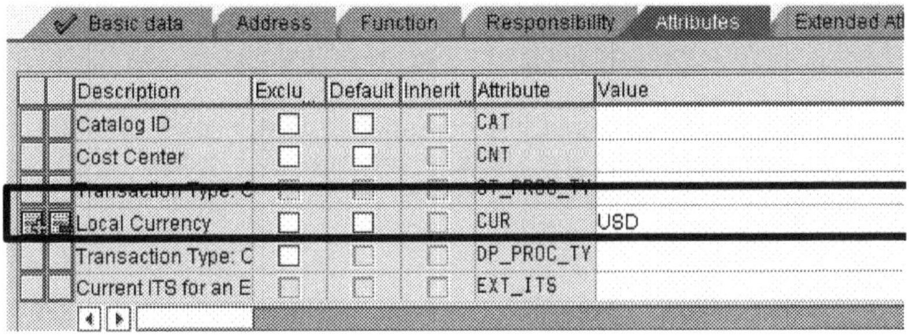

Basic data | Address | Function | Responsibility | Attributes | Extended At

Description	Exclu	Default	Inherit	Attribute	Value
Catalog ID	☐	☐	☐	CAT	
Cost Center	☐	☐	☐	CNT	
Transaction Type: C	☐	☐	☐	BT_PROC_TY	
Local Currency	☐	☐	☐	CUR	USD
Transaction Type: C	☐	☐	☐	DP_PROC_TY	
Current ITS for an E	☐	☐	☐	EXT_ITS	

8.3) Create Users in the Organizational Structure

Team Responsible:	**Functional Configuration**
Transportable:	**No**

Use

In order for users to shop and perform tasks in the EBP Application, they must be entered into the EBP organizational structure. When the user is entered in the EBP organizational structure, they will be assigned a position as well as a business partner number. To perform this task, you can choose one of two options:

1. Replicate the users from the SAP R/3 Organizational Structure (if one exists) to the EBP org. structure via a standard ALE IDoc. Before executing this task, you must perform a series of configuration activities to enable the replication procedure. The replication program is called RHALEINI (Tcode: PFAL) in the SAP R/3 backend system.
2. Execute a transaction in EBP called USERS_GEN which will automatically populate a range of users

into the EBP organizational structure along with their position and business partner.

For the purposes of this document, we will cover Option #2 and describe the steps to add one user to the organizational structure since Option #1 is quite lengthy in explanation.

Procedure

Program Name	*SAPLBBP_MASS_CREATION*
Transaction code	USERS_GEN

1.) Execute transaction code USERS_GEN in the EBP GUI
2.) Select the radio button 'Create Users from existing SU01 Users' and click 'Execute Action'

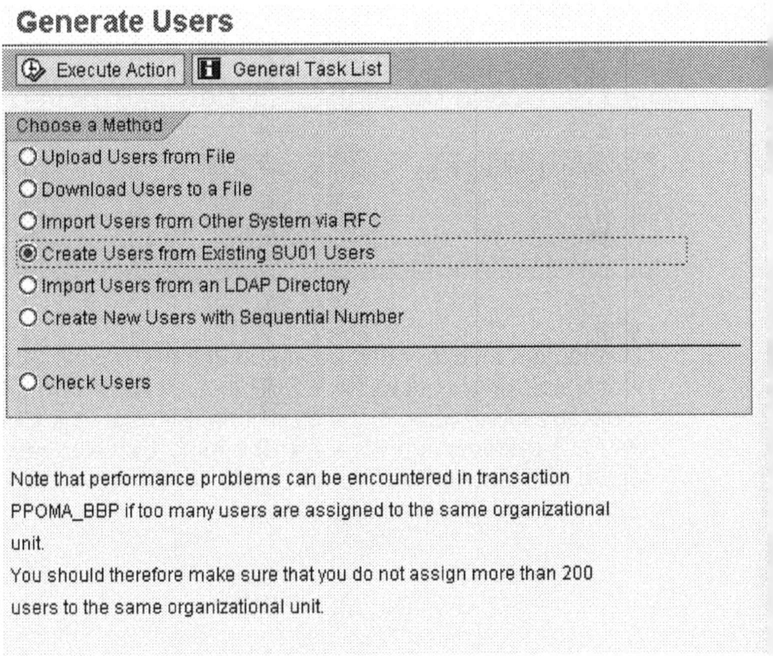

Generate Users

Execute Action | General Task List

Choose a Method

- ○ Upload Users from File
- ○ Download Users to a File
- ○ Import Users from Other System via RFC
- ◉ Create Users from Existing SU01 Users
- ○ Import Users from an LDAP Directory
- ○ Create New Users with Sequential Number

- ○ Check Users

Note that performance problems can be encountered in transaction PPOMA_BBP if too many users are assigned to the same organizational unit.
You should therefore make sure that you do not assign more than 200 users to the same organizational unit.

3.) Enter the Organizational Unit number for where you want the user to reside in the EBP organizational structure and select the appropriate country in the 'Country' field.
4.) Click 'Continue'
5.) Select the checkbox 'Area of Users' in the pop-up and enter the User ID or a wildcard search for the User ID that you want to enter into the EBP organizational structure.
6.) Check the User ID that appears on the search results list and click the 'Green' check mark
7.) The user or group of users will be generated into the EBP organizational structure along with a business partner for each user.

9.) Define Distribution Models

9.1) Define Distribution Models in EBP

Team Responsible:	**Basis**
Transportable:	**No**

Use
Distribution models must be set up in EBP to pass Goods Receipts/Confirmations from EBP to SAP R/3. Two message types need to be distributed between the EBP and R/3 systems in order for a Shopping Cart Requestor or Central Goods/Receiver to create confirmations in the EBP system. The message types are:

- MBGMCR
- ACC_GOODS_MOVEMENT

Procedure

EBP System Configuration
In order to create distribution models and views, you must perform activities in both the EBP system and R/3 system. We will start the configuration in the EBP system first.

A.) Create Distribution Model for R/3 backend

SAP SRM Menu	*Supplier Relationship Management ? SRM Server ? Technical Basic Settings ? ALE Settings (Logical Systems) ? Distribution (ALE) ? Modelling and Implementing Business Processes ? Maintain Distribution Model and Distribute Views*

Transaction code	BD64

8.) Highlight the Model views area and click the button 'Create model view'
9.) In the 'Short Text' field, enter 'Enterprise Buyer'. In the 'Technical name' field, enter 'SRM'. (leave the start date and end date fields as default) Click 'Enter'.
10.) Highlight the Enterprise Buyer and click the button 'Add message type'. Enter the following details and click 'Enter'.
    - Sender: EBP Client
    - Receiver: R/3 Client
    - Message Type: MBGMCR
11.) Repeat Step 3 for a new message type.
    - Sender: EBP Client
    - Receiver: R/3 Client
    - Message Type: ACC_GOODS_MOVEMENT

12.) Click the 'Save' button to save the model view

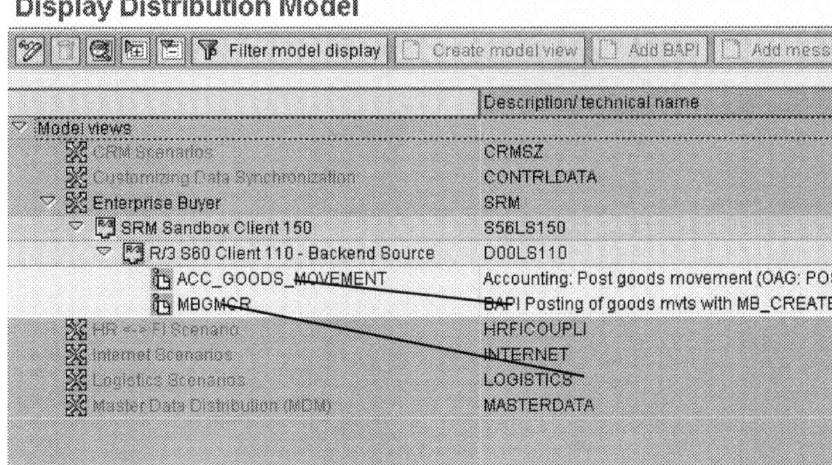

B.) Generate Partner Profiles

SAP SRM Menu	*Supplier Relationship Management ? SRM Server ? Technical Basic Settings ? ALE Settings (Logical Systems) ? Distribution (ALE) ? Modelling and Implementing Business Processes ? Maintain Distribution Model and Distribute Views*
Transaction code	BD64

1.) Highlight the 'Enterprise Buyer' model view and go to the menu path Environment ? Generate Partner Profiles
2.) Verify that the 'Model View' field is filled in with the Technical Name of the Distribution Model (i.e., SRM)
3.) In the 'Partner System' field, enter the logical system name for both the R/3 client and EBP client. Enter both values as 'Single field' values as depicted in the screenshot below:

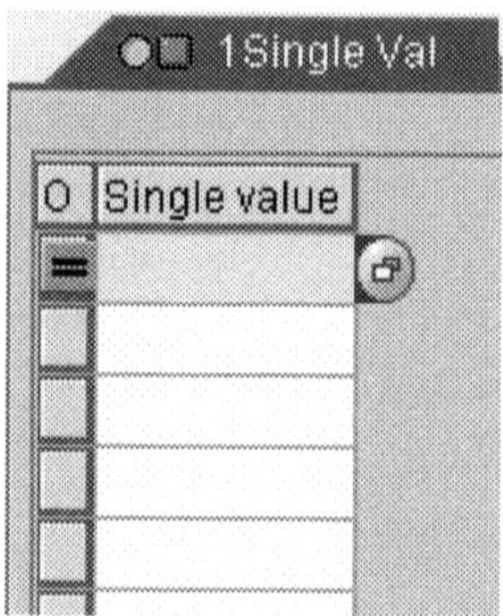

4.) Make sure the 'Transfer IDoc immediately' and 'Trigger immediately' radio buttons are selected.

5.) Click ‘Execute’
6.) A report should be output stating that the partner profiles have been generated.

C.) Distribute Model View to R/3 backend

SAP SRM Menu	*Supplier Relationship Management ? SRM Server ? Technical Basic Settings ? ALE Settings (Logical Systems) ? Distribution (ALE) ? Modelling and Implementing Business Processes ? Maintain Distribution Model and Distribute Views*
Transaction code	BD64

1.) Highlight the ‘Enterprise Buyer’ model view and go to the menu path Edit ? Model View ? Distribute
2.) A pop-up window will appear. Select the logical system ID of the backend system to which the model will be distributed and click on the green check mark to begin the distribution of the model from EBP to R/3.

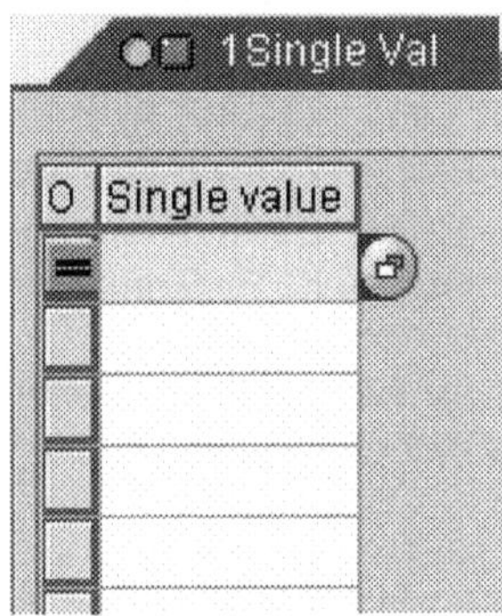

3.) Make sure the 'Transfer IDoc immediately' and 'Trigger immediately' radio buttons are selected.
4.) Click 'Execute'
5.) A report will output stating that the partner profiles have been generated.

9.2) Generate Partner Profiles in R/3

Since the original model view for the EBP generated IDoc's for goods receipts was performed in the EBP system, the R/3 system becomes the receiver to the sender model in the EBP system. Therefore, you must also generate the 'Partner Profiles' transaction for the EBP distributed model view in the R/3 system.

A.) Generate Partner Profiles

SAP R/3 Menu	*R/3 ? Technical Basic Settings ? ALE Settings (Logical Systems) ? Distribution (ALE) ? Modelling and Implementing Business Processes ? Maintain Distribution Model and Distribute Views*
Transaction code	BD64

1.) Verify that the 'Enterprise Buyer' model was distributed from the EBP system to the R/3 system. There should be an entry for this model.
2.) Highlight the 'Enterprise Buyer' model view and go to the menu path Environment ? Generate Partner Profiles
3.) Verify that the 'Model View' field is filled in with the Technical Name of the Distribution Model (i.e., SRM)
4.) In the 'Partner System' field, enter the logical system name for both the EBP client and the R/3

client. Enter both values as 'Single field' values as depicted in the screenshot below:

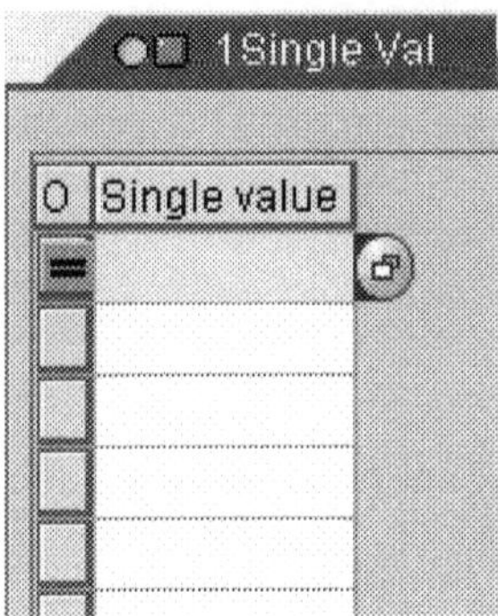

5.) Make sure the 'Transfer IDoc immediately' and 'Trigger immediately' radio buttons are selected.
6.) Click 'Execute'
7.) A report will output stating that the partner profiles have been generated.

10.) Account Assignment Definition

10.1) Define Account Assignment Categories

Team Responsible:	**Functional Configuration**
Transportable:	**Yes**

Use

Define all the valid account assignment categories and sub-account assignment fields which Shopping Cart Creators will assign to for each shopping cart request.

Procedure

SAP SRM Menu	*Supplier Relationship Management → SRM Server → Cross-Application Basic Settings → Account Assignment → Define Account Assignment Categories*
Transaction code	SPRO

Settings:

1.) De-select the following checkboxes in the 'Active' column for the following account assignment categories:
   a. FI – Finances and Funds
   b. NET – Network
   c. SO – Sales Order

Account assignment categories

Account Assignmen	Description	Active	Backend acct ass
AS	Asset	☑	A
CC	Cost Center	☑	K
FI	Finances and Funds	☐	K
NET	Network	☐	N
OR	Order	☑	F
SO	Sales order	☐	X
STR	Generic account assignment	☐	
WBS	WBS element	☑	P

2.) Click 'Save' and enter transport number
3.) Highlight the field 'WBS element' and click the 'Acct. Assignment fields' folder
4.) Click on 'New Entries' and in the 'Account Assignment field technical name' field, click the drop down and select 'COST_CTR' for cost center. Make sure that the radio button for 'Leading Account Assignment' is not selected.
5.) Click 'Back'.
6.) Repeat Steps 4 and 5 for the field 'Asset' and add the fields 'COST_CTR' and 'ORDER_NO' as secondary cost elements.
7.) Click 'Save'

10.2) Define G/L Account for Product Category/Acct. Assignment Category

Team Responsible:	**Functional Configuration**
Transportable:	**Yes, but not recommended***

Save these entries to a transport that states 'Do not transport' or something similar. The reason why you do not want to transport these entries is that there is a

backend R/3 system reference in this configuration table, which will change with each new client.

Use

For every product category and account assignment category combination, define the default G/L account that will be entered into the shopping cart.

Note: If the standard logic is not sufficient to determine a G/L account, there is a BADI called BBP_DETERMINE_ACCT, which allows you determine the G/L account through other parameters besides Account Assignment category and Material Group such as Company Code. For Company Code A, Material Group A, and Account Assignment Category K, you want to have G/L account default as 16300000 but for a different company code with the same material group and account assignment category, you want to default a different G/L account such as 16452300.

Procedure

SAP SRM Menu	*Supplier Relationship Management → SRM Server → Cross-Application Basic Settings → Account Assignment → Define G/L Account for Product Category and Account Assignment Category*
Transaction code	SPRO

Settings:

1.) Click on 'New Entries' and enter the following data:

   a. CategoryID – Material group from R/3 backend
   b. SourceSyst – This field should default in based on the material group selection

   c. AcctAssCat – Enter the appropriate account assignment category (example: CC for cost center)
   d. G/L Account No. – Enter the appropriate G/L Account number in the R/3 backend.

2.) Repeat Step 1 for each material group and account assignment category combination.

10.3) Creating Asset Master Records in EBP

Use

In EBP, Shopping Cart creators can create asset master records directly from EBP, which will then be created in the R/3 system.

In order to activate this functionality, the following prerequisites must occur:

- The Authorization Object M_BBP_ASS must be assigned to the appropriate security role
- The account assignment attribute (KNT) for Asset (AS) must be assigned in the EBP organizational structure for the appropriate user.

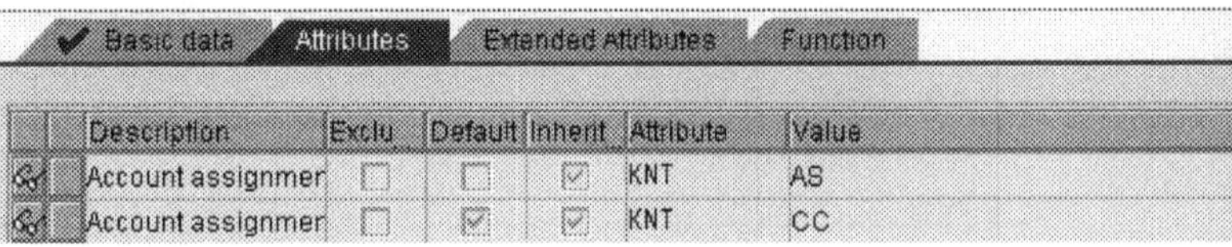

- The Asset Class attribute (BUK) must be assigned in the EBP organizational structure for the appropriate user. The syntax for this attribute is BACKEND CLIENT ID\ASSET CLASS NUMBER (example S00DS100\1000)

11.) Purchase Order Smart Form and Transmission

Step 1: Developing Custom EBP Purchase Order Smart Form

Team Responsible:	**Functional Configuration**
Transportable:	**Yes**

Use

The layout and structure of EBP purchasing documents are developed through SAP Smart Forms technology. EBP provides standard Smart Forms for Shopping Carts and Purchase Orders. The standard Smart Form for the EBP Purchase Order is BBP_PO. In order to develop your custom purchase order Smart Form, you will need to copy the standard form into a new Z form and then call the custom form name through standard configuration. Please follow the steps below.

Procedure

SAP SRM Menu	*N/A*
Transaction code	SMARTFORMS

Settings:

1. Execute transaction code SMARTFORMS in the EBP GUI
2. Enter the form 'BBP_PO' in the Form field
3. Click the 'Copy' icon on the top menu bar
4. Enter the source form as 'BBP_PO'. In the target form, enter the custom name for your form such as ZBBP_PO_NEW'

5. To customize your newly copied form, enter the new form name and click the 'Change' icon.

For more information on utilizing SAP Smart Forms, please visit the SAP Service Marketplace http://service.sap.com/smartforms or the http://help.sap.com

Step 2: Specifying Your Custom EBP Purchase Order Smart Form

Team Responsible:	**Functional Configuration**
Transportable:	**Yes**

Use
You can output purchase orders via the following transmission mediums:

- Print
- Email
- Fax
- XML

Prerequisites

- Vendor Business Partner Records in EBP must be set with a 'Standard Communication Protocol' and default 'Transmission Medium'. To make these settings manually, execute the Manage Business Partners transaction in EBP (BBPMAININT) and edit the vendor business partner record.

Procedure

SAP SRM IMG Menu	*Supplier Relationship Management SRM Server ? Cross-Application Basic Settings ? Set Output Actions and Output Format? Define Actions for Purchase Order Output*

Transaction code	SPRO

Settings:

1. Highlight the row with the 'BBP_PD_PO' under Action Profile and double click the 'Action Definition link
2. Double click the 'Processing Types' folder
3. Highlight the 'Smart Forms Print' entry and click the 'Set Processing' button.
4. Under Print Settings, select the custom Purchase Order Smart Form that you have created in the 'Form Name' field (example: ZBBP_PO_NEW)

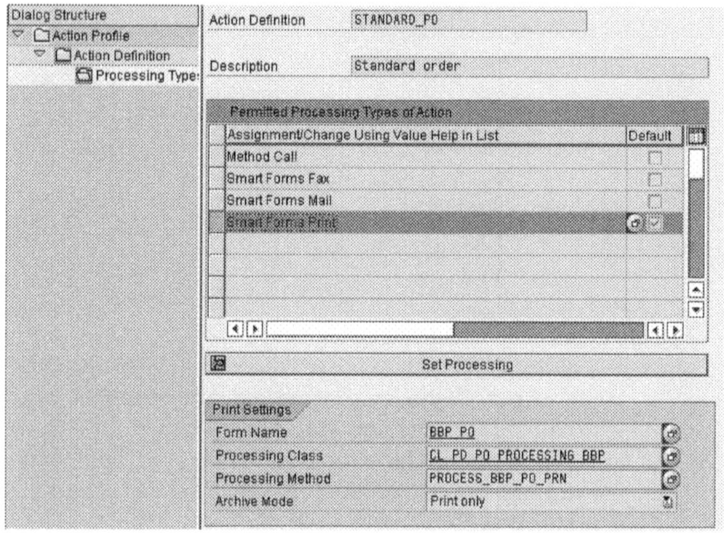

12.) SAP Business Workflow

Team Responsible:	**Functional Configuration**
Transportable:	**Certain Items**

Use

In order to activate the workflow for EBP, the SAP Business Workflow templates in EBP and associated start conditions must be defined and activated for each of the following business objects:

- Shopping Cart (BUS2121)
- Purchase Order (BUS2201)
- Confirmation (BUS2203)

Procedure

Step 1: Verify Workflow Customizing

SRM IMG Menu	*Supplier Relationship Management → SRM Server → Cross-Application Basic Settings → SAP Business Workflow → Maintain Standard Settings for SAP Business Workflow*
Transaction code	SWU3

Steps:

a.) Verify all settings for EBP Workflow are activated and without errors. If there are any inconsistencies in the workflow settings, click the icon to generate the workflow settings automatically or contact the Basis team to perform this task.

b.) All entries should have a green checkmark.

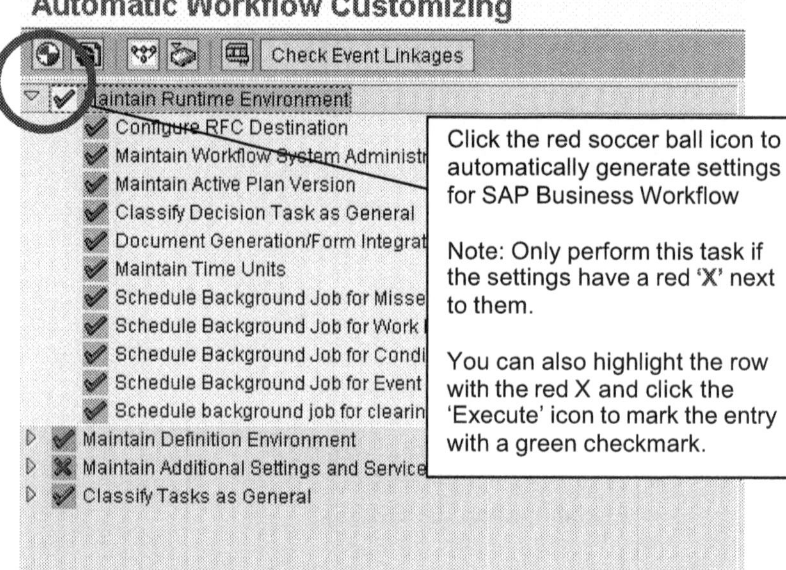

Step 2 Activate Start Conditions for each Business Object

SAP SRM Menu	*Supplier Relationship Management → SRM Server → Cross-Application Basic Settings → SAP Business Workflow → Define Conditions for Starting Workflows*
Transaction code	SWB_COND

Workflow Start Conditions – Define the appropriate start conditions to determine which workflow/s will execute. For example, if the total value of the cart is greater than > $0, start the spend limit workflow (WS10000276)

Definition Area: In this area you can define additional start conditions for workflows or view and change existing start conditions.

The individual lines of a start condition provide the following information:

- Name of the start condition
- Currency
- Triggering event of workflow
- Start condition

List of Standard Workflows in the SRM system

The following (standard) workflows support SRM basic processes:

Workflow for:	Scenario
Shopping Cart (SC) WS10000060 – Without approval, WS10000129 – One-step approval, WS10000031 – Two-step approval	**Approval workflows for shopping carts** The relevant approval workflow is started, depending on the total value of the shopping cart and the role of the requester.

Confirmation (CF) WS10400010 – Without approval, WS10400002 – One-step approval, WS10400009 – Two-step approval, WS10400020 – Administrator approval	**Approval workflows for confirmations** The relevant approval workflow is started, depending on completion status, creator role, and total value of the confirmation.
Invoice (IV) WS10400016 – Without approval, WS10400017 – One-step approval, WS10400018 – Two-step approval, WS10400021 – Administrator approval	**Approval workflows for invoices** The relevant approval workflow is started, depending on completion status, invoice category (credit memo or invoice), creator role, and total value of the invoice.
Purchase Order (PO) WS14000075 – Without approval, WS14000089 – One-step approval WS14000145 – n-step approval	**Approval workflows for purchase orders and change versions of purchase orders** The relevant approval workflow is started, depending on various attributes of the object type *Purchase Order EC (BUS2201)*, for example c*hange of account assignment data*, and t*otal amount difference*.

Purchase Order Response (POR) WS14500001 – Automatic data transfer, WS14500019 – Manual data transfer	**Workflows for transfer of data of purchase order response to purchase order** Depending on the various criteria, the POR data is either transferred to the purchase order automatically or manually by the purchaser.
Contract (CTR) WS14000086 – Without approval, WS14000088 – One-step approval WS14000148 – n-step approval	**Approval workflows for contracts and change versions of contracts** The relevant approval workflow is started, depending on various attributes of the object type *Purchase Contract (BUS2000113)*, for example *change of conditions*.
Bid WS79000010 – Without approval, WS79000002 – One-step approval	**Approval workflows for bids** The relevant approval workflow is started, depending on whether a manager or an employee of the purchasing group accepts a bid for a bid invitation.
Bid Invitation WS14500026 – Without approval, WS14500027 – One-step approval WS14500028 – n-step approval	**Approval Workflows for bid invitations** After bid invitations (and their change versions) are published, one of these three approval workflows is started, depending on the start conditions. The implementation of the BAdI BBP_WFL_APPROV_BADI is a prerequisite for n-step approval.

New bidder/vendor WS10000209	This workflow starts when a bidder or vendor requests a new user for the EBP system.

A selection of other workflows that enhance SRM processes.

Workflow for:	**Scenario**
Spending Limit for SC (one-step) WS10000276	**One-step approval workflow for shopping cart (alternative to SC workflows)** The system uses spending and approval limits to first determine whether approval is necessary, and then to determine the approver.
Spending limit for SC (n-step, dynamic) WS14000109	**Multi-step approval workflow for shopping cart (alternative to one-step spending limit WFL)** Step by step approval of SC depending on spending and approval limit.
Spending limit for SC with BAdI (n-step, dynamic) WS14000133	**N-step approval workflow for shopping cart (alternative to all SC workflows)** Determination of approver occurs dynamically via a BAdI.
Item-Based Approval for SC WS14500015	**Multi-step approval of individual SC items by responsible approver**

Complete SC WS14000044	**Completion of shopping cart by purchaser** Incomplete shopping cart completed by purchaser before approval.
Purchasing Budget Workflow (SC) (Workflow scenario)	**Approval of the SC is not dependent on its value, but rather on the employee's purchasing budget**
Purchase Order Response WS14500007 – Notification WS14500017 – Alert workflow	**Notification when a POR is received and monitoring of POR receipt** As an alternative to the workflow for manual data transfer, (*WS14500019*) the notification workflow just informs the purchaser that the document requires processing. The alert workflow monitors receipt of a POR for a PO where the *Purchase Order Response Expected* indicator is set.
Correction of XML Invoices WS14500020	**Correction workflow for erroneous XML invoices** Erroneous XML invoices are no longer automatically sent back. Now, they can be corrected or processed by the responsible employee before they are posted. The work item contains a link used to branch to invoice processing.

13.) Catalog Content Management

Team Responsible:	**Functional Configuration**
Transportable:	**Yes**

Use

SAP has released a new catalog tool called Catalog Content Management (CCM, current version is 1.0 as of November, 2005) which allows organizations to set up product catalogs from various suppliers integrated with the EBP system. The catalogs can be created to allow EBP Shopping Cart Requestors and Buyers the ability to browse and select items from internal catalogs into a shopping cart request. For the purposes of this document, we will cover how to connect to an OCI or CCM catalog via the 'External Web Services' link.

For more information on the CCM tool, please reference the Requisite/CCM Configuration Guide available at Equity Technology Press (www.sapcookbook.com)

Procedure

SAP SRM Menu	*Supplier Relationship Management → SRM Server → Master Data → Define External Web Services*
Transaction code	SPRO

Define External Web Services

You must define external web services to define the connection to:

1.) **CCM Catalogs** - the Catalog Ids must be defined in EBP for all of the CCM procurement catalogs.

2.) **OCI Catalogs** – All of the vendor catalogs, which will be connected via OCI must be defined within this transaction.

Settings for CCM catalogs:

1.) Click on 'New Entries' and enter a name for the catalog in the 'Web Service ID' field.
2.) Make the following settings:
    a. Description – Enter a general description for the catalog such as Technology Software Catalog.
    b. Business Type – Select 'Product Catalog'
    c. In 'Additional Functions in SRM Server', select the 'Do not check product' checkbox.
    d. In 'Additional Functions in Product Catalog', select the following checkboxes:
        i. Display Product Data Again in Catalog
        ii. Validate Product Data from SAP Enterprise Buyer
    e. In 'Technical Settings' section
        i. Select the following checkbox 'Use Error Log'
        ii. In Logical System, enter EBP logical system
3.) Double click on 'Integrated Call Structure' folder and make the following settings (*NOTE:* The Integrated Call Structure embeds the catalog in the shopping cart window as opposed to the 'Standard Call Structure which displays a pop-up. *The recommended* structure for CCM is using the 'Integrated Call Structure'.)

Note: If you want to enable the cross-catalog search for two or more catalogs, select the 'Cross-Catalog Search' checkbox as well.

CALL PARAMETERS

Sequence	Parameter Name	Parameter Value	Type
10		http://HOST/sap/bc/bsp/ccm/srm_cse/main.do	URL
20	CATALOGID	CCM Procurement Catalog ID	Fixed
30	SAP-CLIENT	Client Number	Fixed
40	SAP-LANGUAGE	SY-LANGU	SAP Field
50	Locale	EN	Fixed
60	CCM-USER	Default CCM User ID	Fixed
70	CCM-PASSWORD	Default CCM User ID Password	Fixed

4.) Click 'Save'

<u>**Settings for OCI catalogs**</u>:

1.) Click on 'New Entries' and enter a name for the catalog in the 'Web Service ID' field.
2.) Make the following settings:
    a. Description – Enter a general description for the catalog, which corresponds to the Vendor Catalog. For example 'ASAP Technology Catalog'.
    b. Enter the Vendor Number in the 'Business Partner' field (the vendor ID associated with the OCI catalog)
    c. Business Type – Select 'Product Catalog'
    d. In 'Additional Functions in SRM Server', select the 'Do not check product' checkbox.
    e. In 'Additional Functions in Product Catalog', select the following checkboxes:
        i. Display Product Data Again in Catalog

   ii. Validate Product Data from SAP Enterprise Buyer
f. In 'Technical Settings' section
   i. Select the following checkbox 'Use Error Log'
   ii. In Logical System, enter EBP logical system

3.) Double click on 'Standard Call Structure' folder and make the following settings:

CALL PARAMETERS

Sequence	Parameter Name	Parameter Value	Type
10		URL provided by supplier for OCI catalog	URL
20	USERNAME	Enter the username provided by the OCI vendor	Fixed
30	PASSWORD	***(This parameter is required only if the OCI vendor supplies a password to you for the OCI catalog)*** Enter the password provided by the OCI vendor	Fixed
40	~LANGUAGE	EN	Fixed

4.) Click 'Save'

In SRM 4.0/EBP 5.0, the following parameters are populated automatically during the OCI punch-out call and do not need to be defined in the call parameters of the OCI catalog:

- HOOK_URL
- ~OkCode
- ~target
- ~caller

14.) Screen Customization

Team Responsible:	**Functional Configuration**
Transportable:	**Yes**

Use

If you need to make modifications to existing EBP transaction and screens, you can use standard technology in EBP to create transaction variants and/or screen variants.

A transaction variant is composed of multiple screens while a screen variant can be called for a specific screen in a transaction or multiple transactions.

Examples of transaction or screen variants:

- Selected fields in the EBP shopping cart transaction sub-screens can be marked as 'Read-Only'
- Selected fields in the EBP shopping cart transactions sub-screens will be marked as 'Required'
- Hiding certain fields and/or removing links to certain sub-screens within the EBP shopping cart transactions

Procedure

SAP SRM Menu	N/A
Transaction code	SHD0

Settings for Creating a Transaction Variant:

1. Execute transaction code SHD0
2. Enter the transaction for which you want to create the variant for in the Transaction Code field (example: BBPSC03 – Shopping Cart – Limited Functions)
3. Click the 'Transaction Variants' tab and enter the name of your custom transaction variant (example, ZBBPSC03)
4. Click the 'Create' icon on the menu bar
5. Create a shopping cart in the EBP GUI (Note: Creating a shopping cart in the EBP GUI is quite more complex than creating a shopping cart using the Web-based HTML templates). Each screen that is executed will open a pop-up screen where you can indicate whether you would like to make a field, field label, or button, one of the following values:
    - W/ Content
    - Output Only
    - Invisible
    - Required

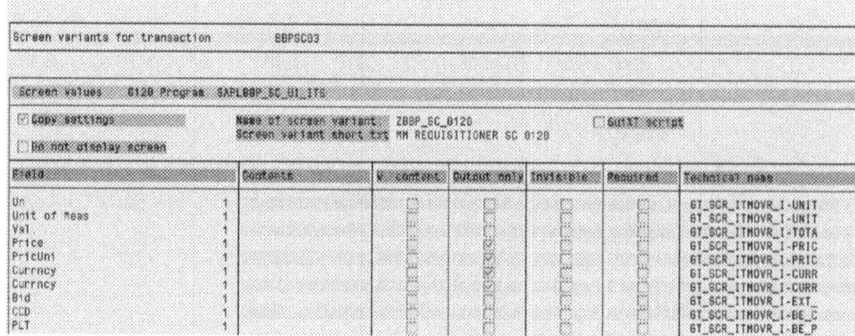

6. If you are finished with the transaction variant, click the 'Continue and Exit' button at the bottom of the last screen.

7. A list of all of the screens that you have executed in the transaction will be displayed. Click 'Save' to save the transaction variant
8. To activate your newly created transaction variant, execute transaction SHD0, click the 'Standard Variants' tab and enter the name of the transaction variant in the 'Name' field. Click the 'Activate' icon next to the field to activate the variant.

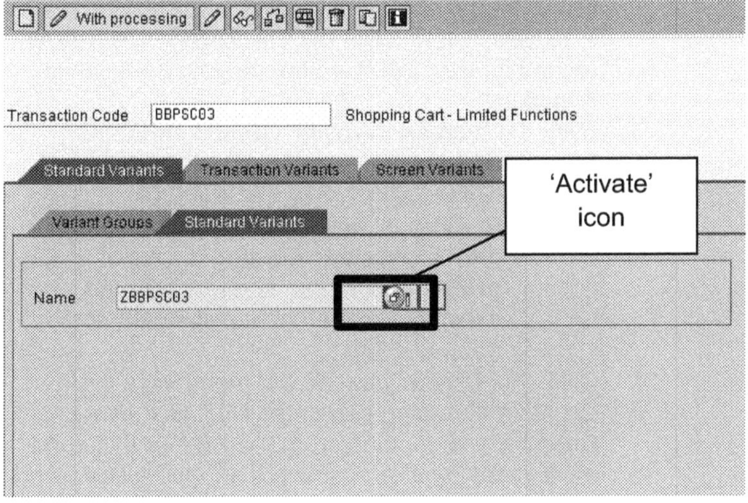

Settings for Creating a Screen Variant:

To create a screen variant for one transaction or a group of transactions which share the same screen, execute the following steps. In this example, we will create a screen variant for the Basic Data screen in the EBP shopping cart line item details:

1. Execute transaction code SHD0
2. Enter the transaction for which you want to create a screen variant for in the Transaction Code field (example: BBPSC03 – Shopping Cart – Limited Functions)
3. Click the 'Screen Variants' tab and enter the following values
    - Name: ZBBP_SC_BASICDATA
    - Program Name: SAPLBBP_SC_UI_ITS (this is the standard program for all of the EBP shopping cart screens with the exception of the cost assignment screen)
    - Screen: 0300
4. Click the 'Create' icon on the menu bar
5. Create a shopping cart in the EBP GUI (Note: Creating a shopping cart in the EBP GUI is quite more complex than creating a shopping cart using the Web-based HTML templates). When the 'Basic Data' screen is executed, a pop-up screen will appear where you can indicate whether you would like to make a field, field label, or button, one of the following values:
    - W/ Content
    - Output Only
    - Invisible
    - Required

6. Once you have created the screen variant, click 'Save'.

TIP √

To call your screen variant, you will need to create a BAdI implementation for BBP_SCREENVARIANTor BBP_SC_MODIFY_UI. Within the BADI, you can call a screen variant using function module RS_HDSYS_SET_SC_VARIANT.

Here is a list of the screen variants provided in SRM 4.0:

Item data overview in an invoice without purchase order reference: BBP_IV_NON_PO
Item data overview in the invoice with purchase order reference: BBP_IV
Item data overview in the confirmation: BBP_CF
Item data overview in the confirmation for time recording: BBP_CF_TIMEREC
Item data overview in the purchase order: BBP_PO;
Item data overview for contracts: BBP_CTR_ITEMLIST
Item data overview for selection of contracts: BBP_CTR_ITEM_SELLIST
Search results for entering an invoice and/or confirmation: BBP_SEARCH_PO
Search results for entering a purchase order: BBP_SEARCH_SC
Search results for displaying/processing an invoice: BBP_CHANGE_IV
Search results for displaying/processing a confirmation: BBP_CHANGE_CF
Search results for entering/displaying/processing/status of a shopping cart: BBP_SC
Worklist for Sourcing: BBP_SOCO_WL
Work area in Sourcing: BBP_SOCO_GA

15.) Additional EBP Settings

Team Responsible:	**Functional Configuration**
Transportable:	**Yes**

There are a number of additional items that you can configure in the EBP IMG to complement your EBP implementation. Among these items are:

- Tolerance Checks (for Goods Receipts, Invoice Receipts, etc.)

SAP SRM IMG Menu	*Supplier Relationship Management SRM Server ? Cross-Application Basic Settings ? Define Tolerance Checks*
Transaction code	SPRO

- Activating Vendor Lists

(Available in the SRM IMG under the Cross Application Basic Settings link)

- Sourcing for Product Categories

(Available in the SRM IMG under the Cross Application Basic Settings link)

Appendix 1 - Important EBP Tables, Function Modules, and Reports

Tables

- CRMD_ORDERADM_H – Purchasing Document Header table
- CRMD_ORDERADM_I – Purchasing Document Item table
- BBP_LOCMAP – Plants replicated from backend system
- BBP_MAP_TAX_CODE – Tax code mapping to backend system
- BBP_PAYTERM – Vendor payment terms uploaded from backend system
- BBP_PAYTERM_TEXT – Vendor payment terms text
- BBP_DET_ACCT – Default G/L account per product category and account assignment category
- BBP_PDBEI – Holds the details of one back-end document such as a Purchase Requisition or a PO.
- BBP_DOCUMENT_TAB – This table will contain any purchase orders in EBP that have failed to transfer over to the SAP R/3 system.
- HRUS_D2 – View a list of substitute approvers for a user.
- T006A – Units of Measure
- TMCNV – Material Master Record Numbers (Max. Length of Material Master Number)
- T100 – List of EBP System Messages

Transaction Codes

- BBP_PD – EBP Purchasing Document Flow (*This is a very important transaction to easily obtain a*

Shopping Cart or Purchase Order GUID and view all of the data, tables, and messages associated with a purchasing document)

- BBP_UPDATE_MAPPING – Vendor mapping to multiple backend systems.
- BBP_ATTR_CHECK (Program BBP_CHECK_CONSISTENCY)
- BBPGETVD – Replicate vendor master records from backend to EBP.
- BBPUPDVD – Update vendor master records from backend to EBP.

Function Modules
(Execute transaction SE37, input function module name, and click the 'test' icon)

- BBP_REQREQ_TRANSFER – Converts shopping cart to a follow-on document.
    - REQNO – Input Shopping Cart Number
- BBP_PD_SC_GETDETAIL – Obtains the Shopping Cart data by using the GUID of the shopping cart.
- BBP_PD_PO_GETDETAIL – Obtains the Purchase Order information by using the GUID of the purchase order.

Useful Reports
(Execute transactions SE38 or SA38, input program/report name, and click execute)

- B_UPLOAD_COST_CENTER_ATTRIBUTE – Upload cost centers to User Ids in the EBP org. structure.
- BBP_GET_STATUS_2 – Report should be scheduled every 2 – 5 minutes. The report always updates all requirement coverage requests (shopping carts) for which documents have been created. Information that is updated includes any follow-on document numbers (purchase orders,

goods receipts, and invoices) as well as the status of a requirement coverage request.

- CLEAN_REQREQ_UP – Report should be scheduled every 2 – 5 minutes and cleans tables of unnecessary shopping cart data.
- BBP_GET_CURRENCY – Schedule this report periodically to update currency tables in the EBP system from R/3.
- BBP_GET_EXRATE – Schedule this report periodically to update exchange rate tables in the EBP system from R/3.
- BBP_CHECK_FRG0060_FRG0061 - Checks if Administration and Master Data (BP Purchasing Fragment) are in Sync
- BBP_UPLOAD_PAYMENT_TERMS – Uploads vendor payment terms from the backend system.
- BBP_CND_CUSTOMIZING_CHECK – Checks customizing settings for conditions in the EBP system.
- BBP_CHECK_CONSISTENCY – Checks consistency of EBP organizational structure including organizational units (departments) and users.
- BBP_CHECK_BP_ORG_ASSIGNMENT – Checks the assignment of Business Partners (such as vendors) and Org. Objects. Validates that the business partners are generated correctly for master data such as vendors.
- BBP_SET_COMMUNICATION_MODE – Sets communication mode for vendor business partners for document transmission.

Appendix 2 – SRM/EBP Transaction Codes

Note: This is not a complete list of transaction codes provided in the SRM system, but does cover a large portion of the important transactions to enable the Self-Service Procurement scenario in SRM/EBP.

BBP0 Start Menu for SAP B2B Procurement
BBPADDREXT Maintain Vendor Address - External
BBPADDRINTC Maintain Addresses for Own Company
BBPADDRINTV Maintain Vendor Address (Internal)
BBPADM_COCKPIT Administrator Monitor Dummy
BBPADM_MONITOR Flow Logic Service
BBPADM_MONITOR
BBPAPPL Define EBP Applications
BBPAPPL_DISP Define EBP Applications
BBPAPPL_TRSP Define EBP Applications
BBPAT02 Parameter ID tree maintenance
BBPAT03 Create User
BBPAT04 Forgotten User ID/Password
BBPAT05 Change User Data
BBPATTRMAINT Maintain Attributes
BBPAVLMAINT AVL Maintenance (Display / Change)
BBPBC1 XML invoice transfer
BBPBWSC1 SC Analyses for Manager (Old)
BBPBWSP Start Enterprise Buyer Inbox
BBPBWSP_SIMPLE Start Enterprise Buyer Inbox (*New EBP Inbox*)
BBPCACC Maintain Account Assign. Categories
BBPCF01 GR/SE for Vendor
BBPCF02 GR/SE for Desktop User
BBPCF03 Goods Recpt/Serv.for Profession.User
BBPCF04 Confirmation Approval
BBPCF05 Carry Out Review for Confirmation
BBPCMSG1 Customizing Flexible Message Control
BBPCMSG2 XML Message Control

BBPPCO02 Purchase Order Response: Entered By
BBPPCO_PO Purchase Order Confirmation: Call P
BBPPCO_WF Purchase Order Confirmation: Call W
BBPPO01 Purchaser Cockpit
BBPPS01 Component Planning for Projects
BBPPS02 Postprocessing Projects
BBPPU07 Manager Inbox
BBPPU08 Employee Inbox
BBPPU09 Administrator Cockpit
BBPPU12 Reviewer Inbox
BBPRP01 Reporting, Data Retrieval from Core

BBPSC01 Shopping Cart - Full Functionality
BBPSC02 Shopping Cart - Wizard
BBPSC03 Shopping Cart - Limited Functions
BBPSC04 Shopping Cart Status
BBPSC05 Public Template (Create)
BBPSC06 Public Template (Change)
BBPSC07 Manager Inbox
BBPSC08 Employee Inbox
BBPSC09 Administrator Cockpit
BBPSC10 Reviewer Inbox
BBPSC11 Shopping Cart Display Item Overview
BBPSC12 Shopping Cart Display Item Details
BBPSC13 Change Shopping Cart
BBPSC14 SC Display for Rec. Management
BBPSC15 SC Display for CFolder
BBPSC16 SC Number of Itm Det. for CFolder
BBPSC17 SC Number of Itm Det. for Rec. Mgmt
BBPSC18 Request Temporary Staff
BBPSC19 Request External Staff (Change)

BBPSHOWVD Display vendor data
BBPSOCO01 Sourcing Cockpit
BBPSR01 Service Entry (Component)
BBPSR02 Entry Sheet Maintenance (Component)
BBPST01 Start EBR Menu
BBPST02 Start EBR Menu
BBPSTART1 FlowLogic Service BBPSTART

BBPSUBSCRIBE Add additional subscriber user data
BBPTRACE Switch on EBP Trace
BBPTRACK Status Tracking: Call Structure
BBPUPDVD Update Vendor Master Record
BBPUSERMAINT user Maintain
BBPU_IAC_TEST Test Transaction for ITS
BBPVE01 Vendor Evaluation
BBPVENDOR BBP Vendor Logon
BBPWEBMONITOR Application Monitor w/o Flow Logic
BBPWEBMON_SEP Monitor in New Window

BBP_CND_CHECK Check Conditions Customizing
BBP_CND_CHECK_CUST Check Conditions Customizing
BBP_CONT_ACTION_DEF Define Action Profiles
BBP_CTR_DISP Contract in Display Mode
BBP_CTR_DISPNR Display Contract without Return
BBP_CTR_EXT_PO Display Contract from PO and SOC
BBP_CTR_EXT_WF Display Contract from Workflow
BBP_CTR_MAIN Process Contracts
BBP_CTR_MAINCC Process Global Outline Agreement
BBP_CTR_MON Monitor Contract Distribution
BBP_CTR_SEARCC Find Global Outline Agreement
BBP_CTR_WF_APP Branch from Approval Workflow
BBP_CTR_WF_CHG Branch Contract from Change Workflow
BBP_CT_SCM_STAGING Staging UI for Schema Import
BBP_CT_STAGING Staging
BBP_CUST_CAT Call Structure Maint. of Catalogs
BBP_CUST_DET_ACCT Determine G/L Account by Category
BBP_CUST_DET_LOGSYS Determine Target System by Category
BBP_CUST_LOGSYS Maintenance of the Backend System
BBP_CUST_TARGET_OBJ MMaint. of Objects to Be Generated
BBP_CUS_ACCESS_SEQ EBP: Define Access Sequences

BBP_DYN_ATTR_EDIT Maintenance of Dynamic Attributes
BBP_EVAL_SURVEY Survey Cockpit
BBP_GETCD_ITS Display Change Documents
BBP_MON Open the Monitor Display
BBP_MON_SC Monitor Shopping Cart
BBP_MS_ACC_DET_C Multiple Company: Acct for Category
BBP_MS_BE_C Multiple Company:Maintain FI Backend
BBP_MS_MAP_TAX_C Multiple Company: Tax Code
BBP_MS_MSG1_C Message Control
BBP_MS_MSG2_C Multiple Company: Flex. Message XML
BBP_MS_STD_ACC_C MultipleCompany:LocalAcctAssigmtDat
BBP_NUM_AUC Number Range Maintenance 'AUC'
BBP_NUM_AVL Number Range Definition 'AVL'
BBP_NUM_BID Bid Invitation Nr Range Maintenance
BBP_NUM_CONF Procure. Confirm. Nr Range Maintenance
BBP_NUM_INV Invoice Number Range Maintenance
BBP_NUM_INVD Number Ranges for Invoice Template
BBP_NUM_PC No.Range Maint. Contrct/Del.Schedule
BBP_NUM_PCO Number Range Maint for NkObj POCONF

BBP_PD_PO_ERRORLOG Starts Entry Screen for Error Log
BBP_PM01 Postman scenario
BBP_POC Process Purchase Orders

BBP_QUOT_EXTWF Display Bid Invitation -> Bid fr. WF
BBP_SC_DARKAPP_IAC Approve Shopping Cart in Background
BBP_SNEW_SYNCVD Shows New Vendor Repl. from Backend
BBP_SP_COMP_INI Replication of Companies & Employees
BBP_SP_SUPP_INI Download Vendors for Service Portal

BBP_SUPP_MONI Vendor Monitor
BBP_SUS_BP_ADM Management of Business Partners
BBP_TRIGG Output Actions
BBP_TRIGG_CTR Output Contract
BBP_TRIGG_ERS Output ERS Document
BBP_TRIGG_INV Output Invoice
BBP_TRIGG_MEN Output Document

Appendix 3 – SRM 4.0/EBP 5.0 BAdI (Business Add-In) List

BBP_ACCCAT_MAP_EXP Exit for changing account assign. cat. by mapping EBP to
BBP_ACCCAT_MAP_IMP Exit for changing account assign. cat. by mapping R/3 to

BBP_APPEND_ITEM Exit while creating a shopping basket item

BBP_ARCHIVING_BADI BAdI Implementation for Archiving Contracts

BBP_ATT_CHECK Attachments
BBP_AUTHORITY_CHECK Further Authorization Checks f. Documents in EBP

BBP_AVL_DETERMINE Determination of Sourcing via AVL

BBP_BADI_SUPP_MONI Activate Customer Monitor

BBP_BID_DET_PROCTYPE Determine Bid Invitation Transaction Type

BBP_BUDGET_CHECK Deactivate Automatic Budget Check

BBP_BUPA_GET_CUF Customer Fields for Vendor Master Data
BBP_CAT_CALL_ENRICH BAdI for Transfer of Additional Parameters to Web Service

BBP_CATALOG_TRANSFER Exit for transferring catalog shopping cart

BBP_CATEGORY_ENABLE Is 'category specials' released ?

BBP_CCM_CHAR_MAINT Transfer Additional Characteristics to SAP CCM

BBP_CFOLDER_BADI BAdI Definition for cFolder Integration

BBP_CHANGE_SF_BID Smartform for E-Mails to Bidder

BBP_CHANGE_SF_CTR Change Smart Form for Contract Output

BBP_CHANGE_SF_ERS Change Smart Form

BBP_CHANGE_SF_POVERS Change Smart Form for Version Comparison

BBP_CHANGE_SF_SC Smart Form Shopping Cart Print

BBP_CHANGE_SSF_ERS Test

BBP_CHANGE_URL bbp_change_url

BBP_CHNG_AGNT_ALLOW Allow Change/Add Approver
BBP_CHNG_AGNT_GET Approver Selection when Approver Changed/Added
BBP_CREAT_RFQ_IN_DPE Change Bid Invit. Data Before Transfer to Dynamic Bidding
BBP_CREATE_PO_BACK Exit while creating a purchase order in the backend syste

BBP_CREATE_REQ_BACK Exit while creating a purchase requisition in backend sys
BBP_CREATE_RES_BACK Exit while creating a reservation in backend system
BBP_CT_PROD_ST_RULES BAdI for Implementation of Additional Product Staging Rul
BBP_CT_PROD_TRANSFER Exit Before Transfer of Product Data to Product Master
BBP_CTR_BE_CREATE Exit when Creating a Contract in the Backend System

BBP_CTR_MAIL_BADI BAdI for Changes Regarding Sending Mails

BBP_CUF_BADI Customer Fields. Call-up of User-Defined Screen

BBP_CUF_BADI_2 Customer Fields. Use of Standard Table Control

BBP_DET_TAXCODE_BADI Exit for Determination of Tax Code
BBP_DETERMINE_ACCT Exit while determining G/L account for account assignment

BBP_DETERMINE_DYNATR Determine Attributes in Bid Invitation

BBP_DETERMINE_LOGSYS Exit while determining target system of item

BBP_DOC_CHANGE_BADI BAdI for Changing EBP Purchasing Documents
BBP_DOC_CHECK_BADI General BAdI in Cross-Check for Message Returns
BBP_DOC_PRINTPROC BADI for Output Processing of Office Document Attachments

BBP_DOC_SAVE_BADI General BAdI for Additional Checks
BBP_DP_PROD_CHK_BADI Exit for Check if Product can be a Direct Material

BBP_DRIVER_DETERMINE Determine Driver Function Modules
BBP_EBPXML_OUT_BADI System Type EBPXML BADI for Outbound Messages

BBP_ECS_PO_OUT_BADI ECS: PO Transfer to Logistics Backend

BBP_EXTLOCALPO_BADI Control Extended Classic Scenario
BBP_F4_GET_ADDR_MODE Should Address Selection Be Restricted to Company?
BBP_F4_MEM_UPDATE Write New/Current Favorites to Function Group Memory

BBP_F4_READ_ON_ENTRY Filling of Input Helps, Initial Defaults

BBP_F4_READ_ON_EXIT Filling of Input Helps, Final Restriction

BBP_F4_SAVE_DB Writing of Favorites for Input Helps to Database

BBP_FAV_DBHINT Determine Whether Database is Called with HINT

BBP_FILE_UPLOAD_BADI Upload File to an SRM Application

BBP_FREIGHT_BADI Treatment of Freight Costs in Tax Calculation

BBP_GET_VMDATA_CF BAdI for Replication of Customer Fields

BBP_GET_VMDATA_IBU BAdI for Replication of Customer Fields

BBP_GROUP_LOC_PO Exit Grouping of Items for Local Purchase Orders

BBP_IV_NUMBER_SET BADI for Vendor Invoice Number
BBP_MESSAGES_BADI Check of account assignment data and message output

BBP_MON_SC Exit for Shopping Cart Monitor

BBP_NONR3_ADDRESS Master Data Handling: Addresses

BBP_NONR3_PARTNER Master Data Handling: Business Partners

BBP_OUTPUT_CHANGE Change Output Parameters

BBP_PC_ACLPAY_BADI BAdI to Fill ACLPAY Segments from PCard

BBP_PD_DOWNLOAD Download Purchasing Document - Renderer
BBP_PG_REASSIGN_BADI EBP Purchasing Documents: Assign Purchasing Groups(s) (SO
BBP_PGRP_ASSIGN_BADI EBP Purchasing Documents: Assign Purchasing Group(s)
BBP_PGRP_FIND Shopping Cart: Determine Responsible Purchasing Group(s)

BBP_PM_COMP_CHK Check and Complete Component Data

BBP_PM_DEFAULT_VAL Setting default values for Component Planning

BBP_PRICEDATA_READ Pricing: Read Price Data (simplified pricing)

BBP_PROCESS_CTR Process Smart Form with Changed Interface

BBP_PROCESS_PO Process Smart Form with Changed Interface

BBP_RESERVATION_GRP Grouping of Reservations

BBP_SAPXML1_IN_BADI BAdI for changing the SAP XML inbound mapping
BBP_SAPXML1_OUT_BADI BAdI for changing the SAPXML outbound mapping

BBP_SC_MODIFY_UI BADI to Change Shopping Cart Layout
BBP_SC_TRANSFER_BE Exit for Transferring Shopping Cart to the Backend

BBP_SC_VALUE_GET Determine Shopping Cart Value for User Budget

BBP_SCREENVARIANT BAdI for Defining Screen Variants
BBP_SEND_MEDIUM_MODE Determines the Default Settings for the Send Medium
BBP_SEND_SUPP_TO_EXT Settings: Send BP from ROS System to External System

BBP_SKILLS BAdI: Create Skills Profile

BBP_SOS_BADI BAdI to Search for and Check Sources of Supply

BBP_SRC_DETERMINE Determine Sourcing for an Item
BBP_STOCH_CUST_BADI Read Frequency, Workflows from Stochastic Customizing

---

BBP_SUS_BP_DUPLCHECK SUS/BP Enhancement for Finding Duplicate Records

BBP_SUS_BP_TAXNUMMAP Enhancement for Mapping Tax Number

BBP_SUS_DOWNLD_FILES

BBP_SUS_FILTER_SCHAR Filter Scheduling Agreements

BBP_SUS_MAIL_DESCR Change subject text for E-mail Notification in SUS

BBP_SUS_QUAN_PROPOSE Default Quantity for Service Items

BBP_TARGET_OBJECTS Exit while determining target objects in backend

BBP_TAX_MAP_BADI Exit for mapping during tax calculation

BBP_TRANSDATA_PREP BADI for processing data in replication/update

BBP_TREX_BADI BAdI for Time Recording (Presets and Time Proposal)

BBP_UI_CONTROL_BADI BAdI for Control of Fields in a Document
BBP_UNPLAN_ITEM_BADI BAdI for Unplanned Items: Screen Control and Presets
BBP_VE_QSTN_DET_BADI Control Questionnaire Definition for SRM Vendor Evaluatio

BBP_VERSION_CONTROL Control: Generate a Version from a Document

BBP_WF_LIST Change Worklists and Search Results Lists
BBP_WFL_ADMIN_APPROV Defermination admin. approver for invoice/confirmation
BBP_WFL_APPROV_BADI Determin. Approv. for n-Level. Dynamic Approval WFL
BBP_WFL_EMPL_WI_BADI Determins Whether a Creator Receives a Work Item

BBP_WFL_SECUR_BADI Overwrites the authorization level of the approver
BBP_WS_AGENT_SEARCH BAdI Determines who can use the Cross-Catalog Search
BBP_XML_CONF_LOGSYS XML Outbound Confirmation: Changing the Logical System

BBP_XML_CONF_SEND XML Outbound Confirmation: Send Document?
BBP_XML_DET_SYSTEM Send inbound XML messages to planning system too?

BBP_XML2PDF Use XML Data for PDF Generation

Shaz Khan

Shaz Khan has been implementing SAP ERP eProcurement and Supply Chain applications for over 8 years. Shaz began his career as a Senior Information Technology Consultant with Ernst & Young and immediately obtained SAP R/3 certification in the Materials Management module. He has implemented SAP Supplier Relationship Management (SRM)/Enterprise Buyer Professional (EBP) projects focused on operational self-service and services procurement, contract management, content management, and spend analysis. He has extensive experience in project management, software development and systems implementation methodologies, and strategic consulting services. In 1999, Shaz helped launch Above Commerce, an electronic catalog company focused on helping businesses establish private procurement exchanges over the Internet. He has managed and implemented SAP and SRM supply chain and operational procurement projects for numerous Fortune 500 clients in the Media, Chemical, Oil, and Financial Services industries including Dow Chemical/Union Carbide, Warner Bros., and Disneyland. He has recently launched his new consulting firm Ciena Partners, Inc. and is currently implementing SRM 4.0 at a major Fortune 100 client. Shaz received his B.A. in Computer Science and a B.A. in Economics from the University of California at Berkeley.

Shaz can be reached at skhan@cienapartners.com

www.ingramcontent.com/pod-product-compliance
Ingram Content Group UK Ltd.
Pitfield, Milton Keynes, MK11 3LW, UK
UKHW041834190726
13854UKWH00002B/523